Journey from Head to Heart

ALONG A BUDDHIST PATH

Ringu Tulku Rinpoche

Edited by Mary Heneghan

Bodhicharya
PUBLICATIONS
Awaken the heart by opening the mind

First Published in 2013 by
BODHICHARYA PUBLICATIONS
24 Chester Street, Oxford, OX4 1SN, United Kingdom.
www.bodhicharya.org   email: publications@bodhicharya.com

Edited by Mary Heneghan
ISBN 978-0-9576398-0-5
First Edition. 2013

Public teaching: *Daring Steps towards Fearlessness*. London, May 2006. Recorded by Bernie Hartley. Transcribed and edited by Mary Heneghan.

Public talk: *The intelligent heart – creating happiness in our lives*. Friends Meeting House, Oxford, June 2012. Recorded by Jonathan Clewley. Transcribed and edited by Mary Heneghan.

Question and answer discussion session: with White Tara group, Oxford, June 2012. Recorded by Jonathan Clewley. Transcribed and edited by Mary Heneghan.

Public teaching: *Meditation*. London, May 2009. Recorded by Bernie Hartley. Transcribed and edited by Mary Heneghan.

Bodhicharya Publications team: Tim Barrow; Jonathan Clewley; Annie Dibble; Marita Faaberg; Mary Heneghan; Maria Hündorf-Kaiser; Marion Knight; Alison de Ledesma; Mariette van Lieshout; Pat Little; Eric Masterton; Rachel Moffitt; Jet Mort; Pat Murphy; Paul O'Connor; Minna Stenroos; Claire Trueman; David Tuffield.

Typesetting & Design by Paul O'Connor at www.judodesign.com
Cover images: © Yeshe Lhadron, Mandala Garden, Holy Isle, Scotland.
Inside back cover image: © R.D.Salga, Nepal: www.facebook.com/ExquisiteTibetanArt
Printed on recycled paper by Imprint Digital, Devon, UK.

The Heart Wisdom Series
By Ringu Tulku Rinpoche

No. 1 - Mahamudra & Dzogchen
[reprinted in Heart Wisdom No. 4]

No. 2 - The Ngöndro
Foundation Practices of Mahamudra

No. 3 - From Milk to Yoghurt
A Recipe for Living and Dying

No. 4 - Like Dreams and Clouds
Emptiness and Interdependence; Mahamudra and Dzogchen

No. 5 - Dealing with Emotions
Scattering the Clouds

No. 6 - Journey from Head to Heart
Along a Buddhist Path

Contents

Editor's Preface

Days are where we live.

The idea for this book came out of noticing how helpful *Thought for the Day* books were to people, and then expanding the *thought* out to a *teaching* – a teaching for each day. While there is a theme running through what is included here, each section is designed to offer a self-contained reading, concise enough that we can bring the influence into our daily lives.

Buddhist teaching is broad and deep, detailed and elaborated in many different ways. Yet there are core themes that run through all Buddhadharma. Sometimes, when we are embroiled in busy lives, it is not possible to study large volumes of teachings in depth, or even to keep reading through relatively small books. In times like this the challenge is to remember the essence of Dharma and keep it in the forefront of our minds as we go about our lives. The living Dharma is, after all, that which we apply in our lives and express as we live.

Ringu Tulku's teachings bring out these common and fundamental threads at the core of Buddhadharma. We have drawn from several of his teachings to compile this set of short reflections. Our main source was a series of teachings Ringu Tulku gave in London in May 2006 entitled *Daring Steps towards Fearlessness*. Ringu Tulku taught on the three main vehicles of Buddhism, taking us through the Sravakayana to the Mahayana or Bodhisattvayana, and on to the Vajrayana ways of practising. If not mentioned otherwise, this is where the extracts included here are taken from.

Other sources include a public teaching given in London in May 2009 on *Meditation* and a question and answer discussion with the 'White Tara Group' and public talk, both given in Oxford in June 2012. The White Tara Group is a practice group that meets monthly in Oxford to listen to Ringu Tulku's recorded teachings, discuss them and practise meditation together. During our discussions we highlight what particularly struck us from the teaching, looking at what it means to us and how it relates to our own life experiences. After listening to the *Daring Steps towards Fearlessness* teachings mentioned above, extracts of Ringu Tulku's words were chosen to include here, based on what the group found particularly helpful.

White Tara herself, who the group is named for, is a female embodiment of enlightenment. She displays the qualities of perfectly realised compassion and wisdom, which mark all those who are fully awake or enlightened. And, within this, the particular blessings she brings out are long life, good health and the wisdom of clear seeing. Ringu Tulku talks about Tara more fully in teachings included here. Because of her particular qualities, White Tara is said to watch over Dharma study and practice and to encourage the conditions that uphold it, which is why we set up the Oxford group under her banner. A section on Tara is included in this book as an example of how a deity can be used in Buddhist practice.

Further information on the topics touched on in these excerpts of Ringu Tulku's teachings can be found in some of his other books. A full elucidation of the three vehicles of Buddhism is found in his comprehensive book *Daring Steps*, edited by Rosemarie Fuchs. The Lazy Lama series looks at key topics like Meditation, Taking Refuge and The Four Noble Truths; in a simple and direct way. More on the philosophy of Emptiness and Interdependence, and the practices of Mahamudra and Dzogchen, are found in Heart Wisdom No.4 *Like Dreams and Clouds*. A step-by-step guide to *Dealing with Emotions* is found in the Heart Wisdom book of that title, No.5. Talks on Death and Dying, Reincarnation and Working with a Spiritual Teacher form Heart Wisdom No.3: *From Milk to Yoghurt*; and further instruction on the Vajrayana practices of *Ngöndro* are found in Heart Wisdom No.2.

We hope you enjoy your reading and these teachings bring benefit into many days.

Mary Heneghan
Bodhicharya Publications
Oxford, February 2013

May all beings be happy and have the causes of happiness.
May they be free from suffering and all causes of suffering.
May they never be separate from great happiness untainted by suffering.
And may they dwell in natural great peace,
free from attachment and aversion.

Fear, Suffering and Happiness

The Buddha Taught Four Noble Truths:

There is suffering.
There is the cause of suffering.
There is the cessation of suffering
And there is the path to the cessation of suffering.

Then he said:
There is suffering; it has to be understood.
There is the cause of suffering, which has to be eliminated.
There is the cessation of suffering, which must be achieved.
There is the path to the cessation of suffering, which must be practised.

And then he said, again:
There is suffering; it has to be understood,
but there is nothing to understand.
There is the cause of suffering, which has to be eliminated,
but there is nothing to eliminate.
There is the cessation of suffering, which must be attained,
but there is nothing to attain.
There is the path to the cessation; it must be practised,
but there is nothing to practise.

Taken from 'The Lazy Lama looks at the Four Noble Truths' by Ringu Tulku

Suffering is based on fear:
Fear of pain brings the suffering
of suffering. Fear of change
brings the suffering of change.
Fear of insecurity brings
all-pervasive suffering.

What is suffering?

When we talk about suffering or happiness, I think it is good to mention the basis of what we mean by suffering and by happiness. When Buddha left his kingdom and his wife and child, it was not because he did not love his wife and child or because he did not care for them. It was because he saw that the people of the world have many problems and pains and difficulties, and he saw that people did not like this; they did not want it. They wanted to be free from these problems and difficulties.

Some of these sufferings people want to be free from are emotional sufferings. Some are more what we could call physical difficulties, like old age, illness and death. Other sufferings are getting what we do not want and not getting what we do want. Buddha asked: "Is there a solution? Is there a way to become free from these problems?" This is what Buddha set out to discover. The search for the Dharma was literally the search for the end of suffering, the search to find a lasting happiness where there is no suffering.

Sometimes I feel that when we talk about this kind of happiness, this kind of freedom from suffering, it is more like a freedom from fear. In Buddhism we talk about three sufferings that most people in the samsaric world suffer from. These three are traditionally presented as:

- The suffering of suffering
- The suffering of change
- All-pervading suffering

When we look at what we really mean by these three things and what they really are, it seems that the suffering of suffering is like the suffering of pain. This includes getting ill, being in pain, losing something that you love or not getting something you love. The suffering of change is that, even though things are okay at the moment, you are not happy because you have the fear that things are going to change. When we look deeply I think these sufferings are actually three fears:

- The *fear of pain* is the suffering of suffering
- The *fear of change* is the suffering of change
- The *fear of insecurity* is the all-pervading suffering

Insecurity is that we do not know what is going to happen. We do not know if there is anything that we can hold on to. Many people, nearly everybody, have this fear. It may not be obviously expressed but deep down we all have it. We all have this fear because we know there is nothing really that we can secure for the future. So there is fear.

These three fears are called samsara. If we are not able to do something about these three fears then we cannot be totally happy and cannot have lasting peace of mind; we can never be completely satisfied, completely content, completely in peace. Therefore, the question is whether it is possible for us to become free from these fears and find a real and lasting peace? [i]

The solution does not come from solving all the problems around us. It comes from learning how to deal with problems from within - learning how to feel peaceful and joyful even when different kinds of problems are going on in life.

Fearlessness and peace

Fear brings so much suffering to us human beings. When we talk about fear and fearlessness, however, we have to be clear what we mean. I am not talking about the kind of fearlessness where you say, 'I am so brave! I don't fear anything!' – a boasting type of fearlessness. Sometimes young people, and sometimes old ones too, they have this attitude: 'I don't fear anything!' I, myself, am from Eastern Tibet. People have this attitude there a lot. Sometimes people boast, 'Even if you hit me, I will not go back! I will never run away!' to show how fearless they are. But that is just a foolish kind of fearlessness and it is not what we are aiming for here.

What I am talking about is a fearlessness that arises because you deeply understand that there is no need to have any fear. You have a real and deep understanding that there is no need of any fear. When that kind of experiential understanding happens then you become free. That is why fearlessness is one of the main things talked about from the Buddhist point of view.

Sometimes Buddha is described as The Four Fearlessnesses. He is completely confident, completely clear and completely certain about things, so that there is nothing left to doubt or to fear. When that kind of deep understanding happens, not only as an intellectual understanding but an experiential understanding; when that kind of fearlessness arises, then it is a very high level of realisation. It brings great freedom. And it brings the greatest peace to yourself.

From the Buddhist point of view, the main purpose in life is for each of us to learn how to bring peace in our mind; and create peace in the world around us. If you can do that, then you have done something good for yourself and something good for the world.

I must say what I mean by peace here also, because people have different views about peace. I was talking about peace somewhere one time and somebody said, 'Peace? It's so boring!' It was a misunderstanding of what I was talking about. Sometimes people understand peace as 'nothing happening, nothing exciting, nothing interesting'. That is not what I mean here. The understanding of peace here is 'no conflict, no disturbance within'. As a result of this peace, you are settled; you are grounded. You feel 'not disturbed, not in anguish'. We could say you feel *satisfied*. You feel balanced and in harmony with yourself, so you feel satisfied and in harmony within yourself and with others.

Within this peace, there is no disturbance. So there is no fear, no anguish, no big problem that you cannot handle. There is no problem at all. This is one thing that I think is very important for us to understand. The solution does not come from solving all the problems around us. It comes from learning how to deal with the problems from within - learning how to feel peaceful and how to feel joyful and how to feel okay *even when* different kinds of problems are going on in your life. Because, if you expect that you will first solve all your problems and then you will have peace, that is not going to happen. So I think it is extremely important to have this deep understanding.

Problems keep arising; they keep on coming. I cannot afford to wait until all the problems are solved before I bring peace in my heart. I have to bring peace in my heart while there are still problems going on. Some of the problems we can solve; some of the problems take time to solve; some of the problems do not get solved. But we have to bring peace within ourselves in whatever situation. Otherwise we will never have peace in our heart. That is the understanding.

When that peace happens, it is not just an 'activity-less peace', a peace where nothing happens. Peace here means you can still be very active. Lots of things can be happening. You can be very active, but still have peace within. Generally when you have that peace of heart, then peace and joy come together. The more peace you have in your heart and in your experience, the more happiness and joy it brings. And the more joy there is, the more you become warm-hearted. The peace brings not only satisfaction and happiness but also more kindness with others. A peaceful mind can have more kind-heartedness and warmth; more willingness to help others and be helpful to others. Compassion arises in this way, as a kind of by-product of the peace.

The more you experience this peace, the more fearless you become, because there is no need to fear. This understanding means that the more you can develop that within yourself, the better it is for you. Because you become more kind, you can also become more joyful. And because your mind becomes satisfied and undisturbed, it becomes much more aware and relaxed. And this allows your mind to become much more creative. The more peaceful you become, the more creative you become as well.

When I can let any experience come and let it go, nice experiences and not-so-nice experiences just the same; whatever experience comes, it is okay for me. When I have learnt this very deeply I can have the confidence that, whatever happens, it will be okay. When I have that confidence then I have peace of mind. I have fearlessness.

Happiness

Student: It seems to me people talk a lot about suffering in Buddhism - all the different kinds of suffering, and how much work we have to do, in every different direction, to overcome this suffering. Can you tell us something about happiness instead?

Rinpoche: Happiness? What is happiness then? I think we have to mention suffering in order to answer that question but, still, I thought I was always talking about happiness! I think happiness is essentially the absence of suffering, but it can be more than that. It is peace.

Real happiness, that is supposed to come from the practice of meditation, is not happiness in contrast to unhappiness. True happiness comes from going beyond 'happiness and unhappiness'. Let us look at what that means. It is why meditation is important.

Happiness and unhappiness are both experiences. The experience could be something like, 'I see this and I don't like this.' Or, 'I have this and it is not good.' I experience this feeling or this thought and if I think it is not nice, I don't want it. That is unhappiness. Or maybe I might think, 'That is very nice. I want to experience it but I can't experience it so it is not nice.' That is also unhappiness. I may have a little bit of what I want but, if I do, I also have the fear of losing it, the fear that it will go away. I fear the state of unhappiness. Our way of reacting is very fearful. There is a lot of fear and a lot of aversion in how we generally react.

It is all about how we experience life. When I experience something unpleasant, if I can deeply, deeply experience that it is unpleasant but it is a momentary experience, it is a manifestation of my mind, which means I can then relax within it; I find the experience comes and then it goes. Because everything comes and goes. There is no experience that remains the same all the time. Experience repeats and repeats but it does not remain the same.

When I can deeply experience that a thought or emotion or feeling comes, and I can relax in it, and then it goes; then I get a little bit of confidence: 'Okay, this moment of experiencing unhappiness or pain or problem, I can let it come and let it go.' It is not a big deal. I can do it for one moment. I can do it for two moments. Gradually I gain more confidence.

Then, when a pleasant experience comes, I can do the same thing. When it comes, it is very nice; it is very good for me but then when it goes it is also okay. I can let it come and I can let it go. When I can do this in the same way for a nice experience and for a not-so-nice experience, whatever experience comes, it is okay for me. When I have learnt this very deeply I can have the confidence that, whatever happens, it will be okay. When I have that confidence then I have peace of mind. I have fearlessness.

That is happiness, because you can transcend good feeling and bad feeling in this way. Other than that, you can never get real happiness or real peace, because if a nice thing happens, then you say, 'Oh, it is really nice. I have a really good situation at the moment. BUT....'touch wood' it will not go away!' You already have a fear. Feeling like this does not necessarily mean the good situation will go away, but it does mean you already have the fear of it going away. However much happiness or excitement there is, whatever you have, it is going to change and you know it is going to change. So, therefore, you are not really satisfied, not really completely happy, because you have fear. And that is what we could call a reliable fear. You have not really attained happiness. You may have a little bit of pleasant experience but it is not real happiness.

That is why I say that the training in Buddhism is to learn how to experience: to learn to experience in a certain way so that, whatever happens, it is okay for me. Whatever comes, let it come, and let it go. When that understanding becomes very deep, and not only intellectual but experiential, then you have learnt how to be.

This is not necessarily very difficult for everybody. It could be easy for some people - some people seem to be able to do it very quickly. There have been great beings who have been able to understand all this just like that. It is not that everybody has to work on it for a very long time. It is like learning anything. If you have the right attitude then it is said that you can learn very quickly.

If there is any possibility to lessen hatred, greed and ignorance, then life within our own heart and our own experience will be transformed, and the world outside will be transformed also.

The causes of suffering

The Buddha said the main causes of suffering are klesha and karma. These are two Sanskrit words. There is a word in English for klesha but there is no other word for karma. It is too difficult to translate. So the English have adopted the word karma and put it in the English dictionary.

Klesha has been translated sometimes as 'afflicted emotions' and sometimes as 'mind poisons'. I like the translation 'mind poisons'. It sounds right. We are basically talking about three main things here: aversion, attachment and ignorance. These are said to be the three basic afflicted emotions or mind poisons. One problem with using the translation 'afflicted emotions' is that people don't commonly regard ignorance as an emotion but ignorance is very much something we are considering here.

The ignorance we are talking about is not simply the ignorance of 'not having information'. This ignorance is more of a confused state of mind. It is an experience, not only an absence of knowledge. Ignorance is a lack of clarity of the mind; it is a wrong perception of how things are including what I am myself. It is included as a kind of emotion here when we are talking about mind poisons, as these three are the main things that must be explained. They are at the root of all problems.

At one extreme, for example, wars destroy the peace and bring pain and destruction to many people, including people from both sides of the war. If we look into the reasons for the war in the first place, we can easily see that there are three main strong causes that bring war: One is hatred. If there is no hatred, there can't be any war. Most of the wars are created by hatred; but not only hatred. Many wars are brought about by greed. Greed is one of the main reasons for a war. Sometimes, also, wars are brought about by ignorance, by misunderstanding, by misguidedness. People create a misunderstanding or give wrong information or have a wrong way of looking at other people. Out of that, fear is created, which brings war and conflict.

When we talk about war, it is on a large scale and something we can all see. This kind of thing happens at the national level. But these same causes also bring conflict in our own lives and in our families. Most problems in life that are created by human beings, whether in our family or our relationships or our country, can very clearly be seen to come from these three main things: aversion, attachment and ignorance.

Therefore, if there is any possibility to lessen these - the hatred, greed and ignorance – then life within our own heart and our own experience will be transformed, and the world outside will be transformed also. These are regarded as the most important and the root cause of problems. It is our state of mind and our emotional state which is the root cause of all problems. How then do we get rid of this? How do we change the situation?

We cannot change the situation just like that, by making a declaration. We could declare from now onwards that nobody will hurt anybody any more. But that wouldn't change anything. The only way to work on it is individually and step-by-step.

It is not something that can be done just by deciding something like, 'From today there will be no hatred, no greed, no ignorance... in London, or wherever.' It would be nice if it could be done like this but we are not dealing with something like that. It is not something that can be easily done, even if we want to do it. Even if I don't want to have hatred, greed and ignorance, I can't just wish it away. It is very deeply ingrained in me. It has become my habitual tendency. And that is called karma.

My future is made now.
My future was not made in the
past; my future is made now.
My present was made in the past.
If I allow my present to take its own
course, without trying to influence
anything, then it will follow the
same course, and I will allow the
past to make my future as well.

Karma

Karma is a way of reacting, the way our state of mind works. It is, and it has been, going on constantly. We have been doing what we always do all the time. We have been reacting with these mind poisons, with anger and greed and ignorance. It happens, not just at the level of my conscious mind, but also at a very deep level in the subconscious or unconscious. So I react in this way and it becomes my habitual tendency. It becomes *me* and I keep reacting in that way and seeing things with that point of view.

This is what karma is: our habitual way of being, something that is totally ingrained in us again and again. So, from the Buddhist point of view, what I am now is my karma.

It's very important from the Buddhist point of view that karma is not a punishment or reward kind of a thing. It is not about things being 'my fault'. It's not that if I do one good thing, then I will get this reward. Or if I do one bad thing, I will get a punishment. It's not like that. It is about causes and effects. It is usually described like this example:

If I get sick, why did I get sick? Maybe it is because...

1. I ate too much.
2. I didn't do any exercise for the last ten years.
3. I have been having big desserts every day for the last sixteen years!

Then I got sick. Nobody punished me. I just created the circumstances that meant I would get sick. It is not a punishment. It is cause and effect.

But now that I am sick, what can I do? We can't just say, 'Now I am sick - it is my karma. That's it, finished.' What I can do now is that I should find a good doctor and ask him or her, 'What can I do now?' Maybe I can study and find out what to do. Maybe I should do some more exercise, or reduce my desserts a little bit. Maybe I should take some medicine or something like that. If I do these things, most probably I will get better. That is the understanding of cause and effect, of karma.

The word karma means 'action'. It refers to the power of action. It means what I do matters. This responsibility is very important. How I act makes a big difference, if not to others at least very much to myself. If we are totally engulfed and absorbed in activities and feelings of hatred and greed and ignorance, it will only lead to problems. We will create problems for ourselves and for others. So we need to do something to free ourselves from this way of reacting. If we can do that, we can become better, as individuals and as societies.

Fear is something we are born with. It is a habit, a habitual tendency, a way of reacting. So we can do something about it by learning how to relax and how to change our attitude towards it.

Fear

Student: Can you tell us something about fear itself, not just from the Buddhist point of view? For example, where does fear come from? Do we inherit it?

Rinpoche: Where does fear come from? It is a way of reacting. But then I have to turn to Buddhism to explain more because when you talk about *why* something is a certain way – *what is fear and where does it come from?* – then we need to talk about a theory of why something is that way. A theory has a philosophy behind it.

The idea in Buddhism is that fear arises because of two things. First, you see something nice and you start to like it and want it and then you want to get it, whether it is a thing or it is an experience. You try to get it, in a gross way or in a subtle way. At this time there is a fear that you will not get it. Then, when you get it, there is a fear that you will lose it. You will then have the fear of losing it until you have lost it! Then you have the problem of grief that you have lost it. This is how it is if you are dealing with a nice thing.

If you find something not nice, on the other hand, something bad or an unpleasant experience, then you want to get rid of it. You try to run away from it. You are afraid you cannot get rid of it. But even if you are able to get rid of it, that is still not the end of the story. You fear it might come back. So then you have the fear of getting it back, and you have that fear until you get it back! The fear is something that is inherent in your reaction. If you react with aversion and attachment, you always have fear.

We need to learn how to get rid of this fear and how to transcend it in a deep way; which means we have to learn how to change this way of reacting with aversion and attachment. This is the whole thing we are trying to learn. We can do this in many ways, of course.

We can use our attitude, for example. Sometimes we have a specific fear, like the fear of flying. Specific fears sometimes come from a certain trauma or past experience, but the most important thing to learn is that fear is not any solution. Even if you fear something a lot it does not help to do so. You can perspire with fear and tremble nearly to death but this itself will not change anything about the situation. We need to realise that however much we fear or however much we worry, it doesn't change anything. It is a waste of time and is of no use.

There is a saying, 'If you are a coward, you die a hundred times in a day. If you are brave, you die once in your lifetime.' That is about our attitude. If you are very afraid, it doesn't help. It is much better to think, 'Okay, I fear something. I fear I will get sick or I will die. But when I get sick, then I have to get sick.' However much I fear it doesn't make any difference. It doesn't mean to say I should not look after myself. I should exercise and have good food and take whatever medicine I need. I should do whatever I can so I don't get sick unnecessarily. But fearing is not a solution to anything. When I get sick, at that time I have to face it, whether I like it or not. But I do not have to constantly fear it.

Student: Are we born with fear?

Rinpoche: Yes, we are born with fear. Everybody is born with fear.

Student: Fear is not just our imagination then?

Rinpoche: Yes, it is our imagination, also. That is what we are born with. Fear is a habit. We call it a habitual tendency. It is a way of reacting. So we can do something about it by learning how to relax and how to change our attitude towards it. That is one way of dealing with it, at a kind of surface level. However, if you really want to deeply free yourself from fear, then you have to change your way of experiencing.

Our true nature is actually peace and kindness, compassion and joyfulness. This is the true nature of our mind. Therefore, it is possible to regain this and experience things in this way.

How suffering can come to an end

The third truth of Buddha's Four Noble Truths is the truth of cessation. And this is extremely important. We have said that karma and klesha are the causes of our problems. If these causes cannot be cured or changed, then we will never be freed from problems, from pain and suffering. If it is our fundamental nature that we react like this - if it is that we were always like that and always will be like that - then nothing else can be done. However, this is another understanding from the Buddhist point of view: that there *is* a possibility to be freed from this way of reacting.

This is the main claim of the Buddha, his strongest promise or declaration. This state can be changed. The main reason for this is because our true nature is not this way. It does not consist of reacting with aversion and attachment, with hatred, greed and ignorance. That is not our true nature. Our nature is actually peace and kindness, compassion and joyfulness. That is the nature of our mind. Therefore, it is possible to regain this. It is possible to find a way to experience things in this way.

The example that is traditionally used is of water. Buddha gave this example right from the beginning. He said that water can be very polluted but it can also be cleaned. It can become pure again, because the water's nature is not the pollution. The pollution is something that is added to it. So, therefore, it can become free from pollution. If the water's nature was pollution, it could never become free from pollution. But its nature is not that, so it can become free from pollution.

In the same way, the true nature of our mind is not with hatred and greed and ignorance and these kinds of things. It is clear. The true nature of our mind is basically clear. It is aware and very clear. It is peaceful. It is kind. It is joyful. So, therefore, this can be developed and the negative things can be cleared from it. And if that is done then you completely change, you transform. You transform for the better. Ultimately, you can become enlightened; you can become the Buddha.

We have to work on our reactions, our emotions and our habitual tendencies. Mindfulness enables us to find out what is happening. Then we can apply whatever techniques or ways we have learned. We also apply them with mindfulness. It is the instrument through which we practise.

Mindfulness

Mindfulness is said to be the only instrument that you have through which you can practise. Whatever practise you do, you can work on yourself only through mindfulness. Mindfulness means 'being aware': being aware of what is going on *and* being aware of what you should be doing. It is a kind of remembering, but not remembering the past, remembering what is going on now and what situation I am in now.

This mindfulness is extremely important because it is how we change ourselves and how we work on ourselves. If I find myself doing something that I know is not good for me to do, first I need to become mindful of it. Then I may see, 'This is not beneficial to myself and not beneficial to others.' And I can ask myself, 'What should I now do instead, so that I don't keep doing this?' You may then still decide to do it but you may think to yourself, 'This time I want to do it too much, but next time I will not do it.' Or maybe you already think, 'Okay, it is not necessary to do this,' and you don't do it.

Mindfulness covers not only our actions but also our reactions: how we react in whatever way - with our emotions or with our body, speech and mind. My mindfulness catches the reactions I make and I may realise, 'There is no need to react like this.' For example, if I react with anger or in another negative way, then I know that it is no good. It is not good for me and neither is it good for others. When I catch it and I know deeply that this is not a useful way of reacting, I can kind of relax and say to myself, 'Let go.'

Therefore, mindfulness is the practice. It is the way of practice, the instrument of practice. With mindfulness, you can bring whatever kind of techniques you have to work on these things. Usually we have to work on our reactions, our emotions and our habitual tendencies, basically these three things. With mindfulness, we find out what is happening. And then we apply whatever techniques or ways we have learned. We apply them with mindfulness. That is the practice.

Taking refuge is about making a decision. It is finding a purpose and a path. The purpose is that I want to be free from suffering and I want to help others be free from suffering also. I decide to work on this.

In order to do so, I find I need to transform myself. This is taking refuge in Buddha. I take refuge in the Dharma, so as to understand how to transform myself. And I take refuge in the Sangha, to learn from people who have experience of the Dharma.

Taking refuge

Taking refuge, from the Buddhist point of view, is an important thing. But it is not only about a ceremony; it is about making a decision. I usually say that taking refuge is finding a purpose and a path. The purpose is that I want to find a way to be free from my own suffering and for others to be free of their suffering and, in order to do that, I need to transform myself.

Going for refuge to Buddha is that transformation. It is the idea that I can transform, and I must transform: I should transform and I must work on that. I decide that I want to transform and bring out my own innate qualities of wisdom and compassion and peace. When this is my purpose, I need to do something so that I can work on it, and that is going for refuge to the Buddha.

Going for refuge to the Buddha is not asking the Buddha to come and help me. Taking refuge in the Buddha means I would like to bring out my own Buddhanature and I recognise that I must work towards that. Making the decision to do this is taking refuge in Buddha.

If I understand that I can transform, this must be because there are other people who have similarly transformed. So I take the Buddhas of the past as my examples, as my teachers and as my inspiration. This is also part of taking refuge in the Buddha.

Once I take refuge in the Buddha, then I must also take refuge in the Dharma. Because the Buddha is not going to come and simply take me out of suffering. I need to do it myself. So I need to take refuge in the Dharma. Dharma is the teachings. It is the path or the 'road map' of how to transform myself. When I say I take refuge in the Dharma, it is not thinking, 'Please Dharma come and save me.' It is not like that. I must understand the Dharma and I must use the Dharma on myself. I must walk on the path. Therefore, going for refuge to the Dharma is deciding that I would like to understand the Dharma and apply it on myself. That position is taking refuge in the Dharma.

Then there is taking refuge in the Sangha. Sangha consists of beings who have experience of the Dharma. It is not necessarily a group of people. Sangha can be one person or many people. Sangha means people who have the experience of the Dharma. So Buddha is the highest Sangha because Buddha has the highest experience of Dharma. From Buddha downwards, anybody who has even a little bit of real experience of liberation, is the Sangha. So when I say going for refuge to the Sangha, I mean I need to learn this Dharma from the Sangha, from those who have experience of it.

Therefore, going for refuge to the Sangha also means I choose to be inspired by the Sangha. I recognise that I need to take in good influence and create a situation where I can be influenced in a positive way. I also try not to be influenced in a negative way. I try to create that kind of a situation for myself.

If I can do these three things, taking refuge in Buddha, Dharma and Sangha, then I am practising Dharma and I am on the path. I am on a spiritual path. I have taken refuge. Anybody who has made this kind of decision to themselves, has already taken refuge from the Buddhist point of view.

Sometimes, then, we can also go and take refuge in front of a lama. Not *from* a lama, but *in front* of a lama. This is very important to understand, because sometimes people think they are taking refuge in a lama. We take refuge in Buddha, Dharma and Sangha in front of a lama, and that is the ceremony. The lama is like a witness. Then we repeat our refuge commitment each day or each time we do a practice session, to keep inspired.

We all want to be able to do what is good for ourselves and others. But in order that this actually happens, we need our mind to be more tamed and not overpowered by emotions, habits and distractions. Meditation offers a training to make our mind more flexible, tamed and obedient; easier to focus where we want to focus it.

Why meditate?

The word meditation, from the Tibetan and Buddhist point of view, has a very strong implication of *training*. Actually, I understand the whole of Buddhist practice to be a training, nothing but a training. It is not a belief system, because you can have different belief systems within Buddhism. It is also not purely a philosophy because you can have many different philosophies within Buddhism too. And it is not a social system. It is a training - training ourselves. It is especially training our mind, in order to train our personality and thus change and transform ourselves.

I think that is the whole point of Buddhist practice and so meditation is a very important part of this. Meditation is not the only thing in Buddhism. Sometimes people think Buddhists only meditate and do nothing else! It is not supposed to be like this. There is a lot of emphasis in Buddhism on doing positive things, helping people and generally doing things that would be helpful for others. Moreover, every school and every stage of Buddhism talks about compassion. Compassion is the most important element of Buddhist training. There is no section of Buddhism that does not talk about and emphasize compassion and teach it.

Therefore, as a practice we try to do positive things. What we mean by positive things are things that are good for ourselves, now and in the long run, and things that are good for others, now and in the long run. It is important to realise that helping each other, helping people generally, is regarded as the most positive thing we can do. In the sutras, Buddha said that if you deeply wish to help someone, even just to relieve their headache, that is a much more positive action than making the greatest of offerings to all the Buddhas. Buddha said this himself and he said it again and again.

But, in order to do something good for me and good for others, probably I already know what to do: First, I need to be a little bit of a nicer person, a little bit less angry and less easily affected by things, less 'touchy'. Then I also have to be less lazy, and more compassionate. Ideally, I would do what I should do, and not be carried away by negative emotions and negative tendencies. Sometimes I might want to do something good but I still don't do it. Why don't I do it? Because sometimes my mind and emotions do not do exactly what I want them to do. I can easily be misled and overpowered by my emotions, habits, addictions and distractions.

We want to be able to do what is good for ourselves and good for others. But in order that this actually happens, I must have my mind more tamed - in such a way that if I say, 'Sit down!' it sits down. If I say, 'Stand up!' it stands up. If I say, 'Do this!' it does this; like an obedient dog. This is what we call training our mind. We need to find a way to make our mind flexible, trained, tamed and obedient. Then it will be easier to focus where we want to focus it.

Our mind is very stubborn. It goes somewhere and then when we want to take it away from there, it won't let go. If we have a problem, our mind goes straight to it and won't stop thinking about it, especially if we think, 'I don't want to think about that!' So we don't know what to do. We end up with a lot of problems, suffering and tension. We know it would be very nice if we could focus our mind somewhere else but that does not happen, because our mind has its own stubborn way of going. Sometimes it is said that our mind is like a yak's horn: a yak's horn is very hard and is bent in a certain way. If you want to try and bend it in another way, it is impossible.

So we need to make our mind more flexible if we want to bring more peace and joy to our mind, and allow ourselves to do things that are good for ourselves and others. We need to train our mind and make it more flexible. That training is called meditation. The main purpose of meditation is so that we can train our mind so that it does what we want it to. If we want to relax, our mind relaxes. If we want to focus somewhere, it focuses there. If we want to react in a certain way, in a nice and kind way, our mind reacts like that. If we wish our mind does not worry, it will not worry. This is the understanding of the main purpose of meditation. If we can achieve this, we become much more free. Eventually this can lead all the way to complete liberation of our minds. [i]

Bring your body to your seat.

Bring your mind into your body.

And bring ease into your mind.

It is not just about sitting, but about bringing your body to your seat, creating the kind of situation or atmosphere that everything else is finished for a while.

Bringing your body to your seat

How do we train our mind? It is not just by force. We cannot force it. If we say, 'You shouldn't do this! You can't do that!' it does not work. Because our mind is very stubborn. So, if we say, 'Don't do it!' it says, 'Why not?' *Especially* if we say not to do something, then I feel I *must* do it! So, therefore, the more you push your mind, the more it goes the other way. Even if we deeply feel that we don't want to do something, sometimes we still find ourselves doing it – once, twice, even three times. So we need to train our mind so that it naturally becomes flexible and trained. But this has to be done in a skilful way, in a subtle and deliberate way.

Meditation is this – a skilful and deliberate, conscious, way of training our mind. 'Mind' here means thoughts, emotions, reactions, perceptions, habitual tendencies; all these things we need to learn to effortlessly control and manage. We need to learn, not in a punishing way, but in an encouraging way, like all training and learning. If we make it too difficult and hard and painful, then we won't want to do it. We develop resistance to it and then we don't do it.

In the same way, we need to create an environment where our mind feels comfortable, pleasant and at ease. Therefore, it is usually recommended when you start to meditate, to find a corner or a place or a room like a shrine room or somewhere like that, where you can make it nice, inspiring, comfortable and be undisturbed. So that you feel good sitting there. You naturally feel peaceful and more relaxed. The first thing is to learn to feel easy, relaxed and good. For this reason, people often suggest practising meditation in a natural environment, in a retreat place or a forest, where there is a kind of solitude and not too many distractions or disturbances. But the main thing is that you need to create an environment for yourself that is comfortable and inspiring.

Then you make the mind less tense. How do we do that? How do we make the mind relaxed and less tense? By relaxing the body. The body and mind have a very strong relationship. It is almost that you cannot separate them. The body is very much a manifestation of the mind. Mind affects the body and body affects the mind. So we start with relaxing the body. Patrul Rinpoche gave what I think is a very important instruction on meditation. He said:

Bring your body to your seat.
Bring your mind into your body.
And bring ease into your mind.

This is what Patrul Rinpoche says meditation is. 'Bringing your body to your seat' means more than just sitting on a seat. It is not completely necessary to be sitting on a seat, because you can be walking and meditating, or standing and meditating, or lying down meditating, or eating or anything else and meditating. It was famously once said, 'If you don't meditate while eating and drinking, you waste half your life eating and drinking. If you don't meditate while sleeping, you waste half your life sleeping.' And so on. It may not always be easy, but you can meditate in any way. The idea is that when we train ourselves we need to create an atmosphere that is conducive to training and our mind is not completely occupied with everything.

To bring your body onto your seat means that for that time that you are doing meditation, you try not to do other things. You are not involved in other things. You take it as a break, not only from all your physical activities, but mental activities as well. It is easy to have a physical break from our work, but getting a mental break is not so easy. Even if I am not doing work, I may be thinking about it or worrying about it and then it is just as tiring as if I am working. Sometimes it is even more tiring thinking about work than actually doing it!

I need to learn how to train my mind to stop working continuously, to stop all its activities. Because otherwise I am not meditating – I am sitting here thinking about everything I have to do tomorrow and all the things going on in the world. And then it is no use sitting there. So, therefore, that part of the instruction about bringing your body to your seat is a very important one, and is very deep in a way. It is not just about sitting, but about *bringing* your body to your seat and creating the kind of situation or atmosphere that everything else is finished for a while. The first and most important point in order to relax is to feel that we have finished all our work for now; we are not doing it now. [ii]

*If we want our mind to relax,
we need to bring it to the present
moment. When we are in contact
with our body, in the present
moment, things cannot disturb
us. We bring ease into the mind
by relaxing it and allowing
it to be as natural as possible.*

*Just be completely normal, but just
completely be NOW.*

Bringing ease into the mind

Patrul Rinpoche's second point of meditation is that we bring our mind into our body. Usually our mind is always busy: busy running after things, busy running away from things, busy worrying, busy fearing things, busy reacting. We have all sorts of reactions and emotions and thoughts all the time. Traditionally we call it 'monkey mind', never being still for a while.

If we want to encourage our mind to relax we need to bring it to the present moment. It is not about making our mind blank. Sometimes people think meditation is about making our mind completely blank. But this is not, in a way, possible. Thoughts come. Emotions come. Sensations come. It is all happening. You cannot stop seeing. You cannot stop hearing. You cannot stop smelling or tasting or feeling.

The aim is not to suspend your consciousness when you are meditating. The idea is to cultivate a *direct* consciousness. It is about being *more* conscious, not less conscious. The point is to be able to be conscious, in a clear and direct way, of *now*. Not going away from here and now; not becoming absent-minded or distracted; not being carried away by lots of thoughts and emotions and reactions so that we are not really being here. We are carried away, at least a little bit like this, most of the time though. We think we have so many things to do, but we actually reduce our ability to do them by being tight and grasping, by panicking about them.

Practising meditation is trying to be in this very moment - *aware, now*. You become conscious of all your senses. You can see – of course you can see. You can hear – of course you can hear. You can smell. You can feel. You allow yourself to be as normal as you can, and relax into that. Just be completely normal but just completely be *now*. And be easy in that, and relaxed. Bringing the mind into your body means that when your mind is in the body, then you actually *feel*. You are in contact with your body, in the present moment. You see what you see. You hear what you hear. Otherwise you are kind of 'absent, distracted, scatty.' Meditation is an important training to become aware of what is going on now.

When you are in the present moment things cannot disturb you. If you can truly be here and now, in this very moment, there is no tension. There is no need to run after or run away from anything. Things come and go but how would they disturb you? Disturbance comes when you think about things and put this and that together and think it should be like this and it should not be like that...and so on. All these concepts are what disturb us.

All tensions arise about the past and the future. All tensions and fears and worries are about the past and future. All these are conceptual. They are not direct. When I worry, I worry about what is going to happen tomorrow or the day after. I am thinking about things that *may* happen, are likely to happen, should happen. All my problems are associated somehow with the past, with thinking over how things were: 'That was like that, and that was like that...' This is useless too, because it is not there now, it is finished.

Why suffer from the baggage of the past, which I unnecessarily carry, myself? And why suffer from the future, which is not there and may not happen? But most of our problems do come from exactly here. All the tensions, all the emotions and negative things all come from here. There is no use in this. It does not mean we should never think or make plans. If you want to make a plan, make a plan. Of course, think as much as you want and as much as you need to. But remember, you don't need to think all the time. Also, there is nothing wrong with remembering the past. Remember the past as much as you want to, but not all the time.

The technique of meditation is just to relax in the present moment, with all the senses open and clear. You are alert and awake. It is not that you have to make the senses dull; they should be as clear as possible, but relaxed. In the beginning this is something we have to get used to because our mind is out of control and we can't sit still for any length of time.

But we all want to relax. We don't like having tension and burdens. So, I invite you to feel peace; feel okay; feel your body and mind to be at peace. Develop that sensation. If you feel your muscles are tense, loosen those muscles. It is not easy - it is a practice. Letting be is not easy, so we have to *learn* how to let be. If we can let be, then we are at ease. So, let yourself be. Feel secure. Feel protected. Be aware and natural. Be aware and allow things. Be aware and let be. [ii]

Bodhicitta, most precious aspiration,
May it blossom in every heart.
Never waning, may it flourish and grow
Ever higher and greater.

Bodhisattva
Activity

Anybody who has Bodhicitta is a Bodhisattva. Bodhicitta is the heart essence of the Buddha, of enlightenment, which is compassion - compassion imbued with wisdom. Anybody who has this heart intention is a Bodhisattva.

What is a Bodhisattva?

The Mahayana [literally, *Great Vehicle*] is sometimes called the Bodhisattvayana because this is the Buddhist vehicle that clearly explains what it is to be a Bodhisattva. It is the path a Bodhisattva takes. This is in addition to the general and foundational Buddhist teachings, which the Bodhisattvayana also includes. Mahayana Buddhism is nothing other than this. If we want to talk about the Mahayana, we have to talk about what a Bodhisattva is.

The basic characteristic of a Bodhisattva is compassion. They say anybody who has Bodhicitta is a Bodhisattva. What is Bodhicitta? Bodhicitta is a Sanskrit word. 'Bodhi' comes from the root *Bodh*, which means 'to know, to have the full understanding'. 'Citta' is heart, or heart and mind. Citta is not referring really to the thinking mind. It is more a heart feeling. Someone who has the heart essence of the Buddha, of enlightenment, has Bodhicitta. In a practical sense, Bodhicitta is compassion. It is compassion with a sense of wisdom.

Bodhicitta is compassion with two aspects or two purposes. One aspect is about sentient beings: you see the problems and suffering of sentient beings and you wish that they do not have those sufferings and pain and problems. They, as well as yourself, do not want those sufferings. That is the compassionate aspect. The second aspect, which is also very important, is that I want them to be free from suffering *and there might be a possibility of that.* That is the wisdom aspect.

These two aspects are extremely important because otherwise, when I see lots of pain and problems for other people, it becomes too much for me. I become lost and discouraged, dejected and hopeless; it is just too painful. That is not the case with this kind of compassion. Though it is necessary to work on it, there must be a possibility to transform and solve this problem. When this possibility is there, compassion is not just about suffering and concentrating on the suffering. It is about concentrating on a way out of suffering. This type of compassion is Bodhicitta.

When we talk about the Mahayana we talk a lot about compassion and sometimes people get the impression that in the Sravakayana, or the foundational vehicle of Buddhism, compassion is not so important. It is absolutely not so. It would be completely wrong to see it like that. There is no teaching of Buddha that does not talk about compassion. It is the focus of all Buddha's teachings. So what is it that is special when we talk about compassion in the Mahayana? What is special about a Bodhisattva?

The special thing here is that I make a specific commitment, here, myself. It is not only that I wish everybody to be free from suffering. It is not only that I pray for that or want it to be like that. It is that I, myself, make a personal commitment that I will work on this. I would like to work towards it myself. That is what makes the difference. The difference is a personal commitment to working towards the freedom from suffering for beings; to bring the highest well-being and happiness to all sentient beings.

Therefore, the ideal compassion or ideal Bodhicitta is said to have four types of limitlessness:

- The first limitlessness is that I wish to extend this wish for beings to be free from suffering to all and every kind of suffering: the gross sufferings, the subtle dissatisfactions and all the kinds of things like that, freedom from all kinds of sufferings.
- The second limitlessness is that the wish is extended to every being, not limited to a certain number or certain groups or certain types of being. The wish is extended to every type of being without leaving anybody out.
- The third one is that I not only wish all these beings to be completely free from all types of sufferings, that is not enough. I do not wish that I have the most wonderful and highest kind of happiness and

joy and then everybody else is just free from suffering. I wish each and every sentient being the highest kind of joy and peace that it is possible to get. I wish that for every being.

- Lastly, it is not that I wish them this kind of joy just for a short time. I wish that for all the beings for all time: lasting peace and happiness for all sentient beings.

When that kind of commitment is my purpose, then I am a Bodhisattva. Whoever has that kind of agenda, that person is a Bodhisattva. It doesn't matter what kind of philosophical view he or she holds or does not hold; or whatever kind of man or woman or animal or heavenly being or spirit he or she is. It doesn't matter if he or she is Buddhist or Hindu or Christian or whatever. Anybody who has that kind of dedication and compassion is called a Bodhisattva. The key thing is having compassion and wisdom together.

The wish and the prayer of the Bodhisattva is also that I may be able to help beings life after life after life. So that, if it is necessary and helpful for me to become a human being to do this, let me be reborn a human being. If it is necessary or helpful for me to become an animal, let me become an animal. If it is helpful for me to become a teacher, let me become that; whatever will help. This principle is clearly shown through the Jataka Tales about all the past lives of the Buddha.

When we deeply understand 'what I am', then we understand what everything is, because 'everything' is my experience of everything. That understanding, from the Buddhist point of view, is called wisdom. It is a way of experiencing what I really am.

The right way of seeing things

The right view is very important from the Buddhist point of view. 'Right view' means 'the way we see things' - the way we see ourselves; the way we see the world; the way we understand things. It is also our attitude: how we see things and how our attitude is. This is extremely important because it forms a lot of how we react. If we have a compassionate attitude, for instance, then our way of doing things will be different from if we have a selfish attitude, and so on. Attitude is extremely important. So, therefore, the way of seeing things is extremely important. This means, not only how we see things intellectually, but also how we see things *experientially*.

The most important thing from the Buddhist point of view is understanding 'what am I?' Not 'who am I?' But 'what am I?' What is it that I call 'myself'? It is an on going practice to look at this and maybe it seems a bit of a complicated thing, but it is the most important thing to discover. It is understood that, really, true fearlessness can only happen when you deeply, deeply understand 'what am I?'

When I can deeply, deeply understand what I am, then I know there is no need to be afraid. There is no need to hold on to things. There is no need to react in this way of aversion and attachment. We don't need to run away and run after things all the time. When we deeply understand 'what I am', then we understand what everything is, because everything is my experience. That understanding, from the Buddhist point of view, is called wisdom. It is a way of experiencing what I really am.

This wisdom is sometimes called 'knowing one: knowing everything.' Generally we could talk about two ways of knowing. One way is knowing everything but knowing nothing. The other way is knowing one thing and, through that, knowing everything. Knowing everything but knowing nothing is when you know lots of facts about things. You have knowledge about everything but you don't know yourself; so you still kind of 'run, run, run.' You cannot really solve your problems. You may have lots of knowledge but sometimes that knowledge can even become dangerous - if you are not compassionate enough and you have lots of negative emotions. This is how technology can be, for instance. It is not that there is anything wrong with the technology but if you are a negative person you can use it in a negative way. If you are a positive person, then you can use it for positive things. Any kind of knowledge or power can be dangerous as well as useful.

However, if you were to deeply, deeply understand yourself, that is an understanding or experience that would bring liberation. This is why Buddhism says the view is the most important thing. And there are lots of studies aimed toward finding the right view, to study and to reflect on it. Meditation is regarded as a way of bringing this wisdom out. Because this kind of knowing is not just an intellectual thing that you can understand when you receive teachings and read books. That may only give a conceptual understanding of how I am and how things may be, which is not an experiential understanding.

To get an experiential understanding you have to go deep into yourself and learn how to bring your awareness and mindfulness to the unconscious level of your consciousness. This is the place from which you can deeply experience. It is a matter of 'heart' rather than 'head'. Sometimes it is said that the longest journey is from your head to your heart. Which is what we mean when we talk about developing the right view and understanding it experientially. It is on going, to work on this, and it is very important.

It is extremely important to understand action and its result, yourself.

Discipline is allowing yourself to do those things that you know are good for you. And allowing yourself not to do those things that you know are bad for you.

Discipline

As we work on our view, it doesn't mean that other things cannot also be focussed on as we go. The Buddha gave the whole Eightfold Path which includes also right thought, right speech and right action. These are the main three things: we have to be careful about what we do, how we speak and how we think in order to make sure the way we act with our body, speech and mind is not harmful to ourselves or others. In our daily life, we try to reduce actions that bring harm to ourselves and / or others, as much as possible. And we try to increase those actions that bring benefit to ourselves and others, as much as possible. This is very important from the Buddhist point of view.

This is a morality or an ethics, you could say, but it should be based on understanding. It is not a command that you have to do this or you have to do that; you cannot do this or you cannot do that. It is not meant to be taken like that. It is extremely important to understand action and its result, yourself. It is usually like this in life. If somebody says, 'Don't do that!' We usually feel more like doing it! 'Why not?' So it is important to understand the relationship between things, between our actions and their results. If someone says, 'Don't touch the fire because you will get burned,' maybe the first time you will still touch it a little bit. If you get a little bit burned, then you will say, 'Okay, this is not good for me,' and you won't touch it after that. The aspect of understanding is extremely important. For example, understanding that if I do this and this, it is not good for me and not good for others.

Then I need to allow myself not to do it, because I don't want to be hurt. If it is something that is good for me and good for others, then I need to understand that and understand the connection. Discipline is very important from the Buddhist point of view. And that is what discipline is: allowing myself to do those things that I know are good for me. And allowing myself not to do those things that I know are bad for me. That is discipline. If you don't connect it like this, then it becomes very difficult. But if you understand how your actions affect yourself and others, and connect that understanding with your action, it becomes easier to do the things that are good for yourself and others.

You have to look after yourself in order to help other beings. That is why it is said that the way to generate compassion is through a compassionate way of living. This has to be gradually cultivated, which includes being careful and protecting yourself. The example given is of growing a fruit tree.

Growing a good fruit tree

Whether someone is a 'good' person or a 'bad' person, comes down to whether that person has compassion or not. If a person only thinks about their own welfare and profit and does not think about the welfare, profit and concerns of others at all, that person is destructive to the world and to their environment. They are not a very useful or beneficial person. And they are not very beneficial to themselves either. Because, if I only do supposedly good things for myself and, in the process, I harm others, it will not be good for me in the end either.

However, the idea is not that I only care for others and I don't care for myself. Sometimes compassion is seen like that - that it is about being completely selfless and only doing things for others; that you have to sacrifice yourself all the time and you should not look after yourself any more. That is not the idea. That is not what compassion is. You have to look after yourself. If you don't look after yourself, who will look after you? But you look after yourself *in order to help other beings*.

That is why it is said that the way to generate compassion is through a compassionate way of living. This has to be gradually cultivated, which includes being careful and protecting yourself. The example given is of growing a fruit tree.

If you want to grow a good fruit tree, how do you do it? First you have to plant the seed. Maybe you plant it in a pot. You have to bring the right kind of soil and manure, the right kind of mixture, and then put it in a pot. Then you plant the seed in the pot and see that it is watered properly and it has enough sun. Maybe you take it outside in the daytime and put it inside at night time. You make sure that frost does not harm it. You really take care. Otherwise it will not grow, the seed would be finished.

In the same way, it is said that when you are somebody who is generating Bodhicitta and is working on this kind of a compassionate way of life, it is not that you do not need to look after yourself. You should look after yourself *very much*. Your compassion has to be very much protected. You don't need to do anything that would injure yourself. If somebody asks you to do something, then you have to see whether it is good for yourself to do it, and whether it is good for others.

'Something good for yourself' means something that is good for yourself now and also good for yourself later on. If it is only good for you now, it may be enjoyable, but if after some time it would bring some problems, then it is not really good for you. It is the same for things that are good to do for others, also. 'Good for yourself and good for others' means it brings a pleasant result, peace of mind and causes a certain kind of long term happiness and benefit, for myself and for others. That is what we try to work on. It is the same as the Eightfold Path.

If it is good for yourself and good for others, then why not do it? Then you can do it as much as you like! But if it is not good for yourself and is only good for others, then you have to see if it is *okay* for you to do it or not. You have to see whether you can do it without sacrificing too much, without losing your own stability. You have to see whether you would regret it. If you would regret it later, then you should not do it. Then it is something you still need to work on, to strengthen yourself. This is trying to see, in a proper way, that what you do does not disturb or harm yourself, as well as not harming others. It is like planting the seed in a good plant pot and taking care of it.

Then that plant will grow. As it grows a bit more, then what would you do? You would take it and plant it outside, in the garden. You still have to protect it. You might put a little fence around it so cows and sheep don't come and eat it, and nobody walks into it. You would see that it is still protected, but it doesn't need as much protection as earlier. In the same way, when your compassion becomes stronger, and your wisdom becomes stronger, then it is less necessary to protect it. Still, you have to protect it a bit. You make sure that you don't do too much and you take time to re-inspire yourself and things like that.

Then your compassion and wisdom will grow stronger and stronger, like a bigger and bigger tree. Maybe you won't need that protection so much anymore. The tree might not need the fence any longer. The cows cannot eat the tree now. You still have to be a little bit careful at this stage. But then the tree becomes a big tree. And then you don't need to do anything. You can just sit under it and enjoy its shade. You open your mouth and the fruits simply fall into it!

This is the idea. When you first generate Bodhicitta, you first protect yourself. You protect your own interests. You do something that is good for you and good for others, not just good for others. If something is good for others, then the practise is to see how much you can do it. You try to see where the balance is and slowly, slowly you generate Bodhicitta in this way. That is why there are lots of practices on this. It is very important from the Buddhist point of view. We generate compassion but, like everything else, it is something we need to cultivate and work on over time.

If you don't have a certain amount of dedication or commitment, then you can never achieve anything really worthwhile. But how to make that effort is very important, because if you make it in too tight a way it becomes drudgery. Diligence is not pushing yourself hard, but motivating yourself in such a way that you become joyful in doing positive things.

Taking practice like a hobby

Right effort is said to be very important because usually we have to put effort into anything we do. We have to work hard. Anything that is important and we need to achieve, we have to do with effort and hard work. If you don't have a certain amount of dedication or commitment, then you can never achieve something really worthwhile or something great. But *how* to make that effort is said to be very important. Because if you make it in too 'tightened up' a way - too much like 'I *have* to do this' - it makes it too much like drudgery.

Right effort is to learn to like what we are doing. We need to learn to like 'positive doing'. That is why it is said that diligence is joy in doing positive things. Diligence is not pushing yourself hard, but motivating yourself in such a way that you become joyful in doing positive things. So, therefore, right effort is not about being hard on yourself but about bringing interest and motivation to doing positive things. It is doing things in an interested and motivated way.

I usually think about the word 'hobby' when I talk about this. When I first heard the word 'hobby' we were studying English at a time when nobody knew English in Tibetan society. So we had English teachers who did not know Tibetan at all. When I first studied English, there was not a single Westerner who knew one word of Tibetan. None of my teachers knew any word of Tibetan or anything like that. In one way it was hard. But in another way it was very good. One should learn a language in that way, I think. When your parents teach you language originally, it is not done through translation, is it? So our English teachers had to bring things to show us the meaning of words. They said 'grass' and then they brought some grass. And we would say, 'Oh, yes, grass, *grass!*'

We did not understand the word 'hobby' though: 'Hobby? What is your hobby?'

'What do you do when you don't have anything to do?'

'What do I do when I don't have anything to do? – I don't do anything!'

We Tibetans have never had any hobbies. We didn't have this concept at all. But I like the idea - something that you do when you don't do other things, when you are not doing work. You are very inspired by doing it and you never get tired doing it. It could be hard work - it doesn't matter. It could be expensive - it doesn't matter. It could be dangerous - it doesn't matter. It's fantastic. So I have always thought that if you could take practice like a hobby, that is right effort. And that is how we can try to take any practice in the right way.

Suffering alone does not necessarily get rid of negative karma. More and more negativity is easily created when we are suffering. In order to get rid of negative karma and gain something positive, we must actually start being positive. We must start acting positively and feeling positive. We must do things with our body, speech and mind, carefully and mindfully, to cultivate this.

Suffering itself does not end suffering

We have been in samsara for so long, for so many lifetimes, countless lifetimes. There must by now be some kind of a 'store' of so many negative actions that we have committed since beginningless time. If I would need to go through the results of all those negative actions I have done, I cannot but accept that I will have to be in this samsaric, negative, problematic state of suffering for a long, long time.

So if I have the opportunity and freedom, as this precious human life gives us, to purify this and get out of that way of being and create a new beginning, I must totally dedicate myself towards that. I must be extremely mindful and extremely careful that I actually take action in this and not delay. I must not be lazy or ignorant and just let it go by.

The 22nd verse of Chapter 4 of the Bodhicharyavatara says: 'Mere experience of such pain does not result in being freed from it.'

I may think, 'I have lots of pain and I have suffered a lot before. Maybe I will be propelled to different kinds of negative realms and then I will suffer more to the point where, finally, all this negativity will be finished...' But, according to the Buddhist way of understanding, that is not correct. It is not just suffering that gets rid of our negative karma or negative actions. The reason why is given in the Bodhicharyavatara next: 'For in the very suffering of such states, more evil will occur, and then in great abundance.'

When we are suffering and we are in a negative state, our negative actions actually grow. Many negative emotions will come. Negative actions or negative karma are not just created as one negative action and then, while we are going through the result of that, we don't accumulate any further negativity. That is not true - because when we are suffering, then we get angry, we get annoyed, we get upset. So, therefore, it actually goes on and on. More and more negativity is created. Suffering alone does not necessarily get rid of negative karma.

In order to get rid of negative karma and in order to gain something positive, we must actually start *being* positive. We must start acting positively and feeling positive. We must do things with our body, speech and mind, carefully and mindfully, to cultivate this and accumulate positive actions and experiences and change the pattern. This is extremely important. [iii]

It is extremely important not to only concentrate on problems. We have to solve the problems we have, if we can, but there are always many other things going on even while we have problems. It helps more if we feel positive than if we allow our mind to focus only on our problems, clamped onto them like a crocodile.

How to be with our problems

It is very important to concentrate on positive things and not just negative things. Generally each of us experiences many problems. When we have a problem our mind focuses on it to the point that it becomes difficult to get rid of that problem from our mind for even a few seconds. We think, 'I have this problem....I have this problem...Until this problem is solved, I cannot do anything. I cannot think about other things. I cannot enjoy my life. Only if this problem is solved, then I will be happy. Then I will rejoice. Then I will enjoy my life. Then I will do something very nice.' That is our way of thinking.

Then, just as we get that problem solved, two more come along! We think, 'Ah, that is too bad. I just solved that problem and then I was really going to enjoy my life forever.' Even if those two problems are just nearly solved, what happens then? Three more problems come along.

If I live my life going from problem to problem like that, then what would be the state of my mind when I am a little bit older?

Grumpy old man!

What else can you expect?

So therefore, it is extremely important not to concentrate only on our problems. Of course we have to solve the problems if we can, yes, but there are always many other things going on as well as our problems. Generally, though, we can't manage to detach ourselves from the problems at all. We are like a crocodile, clamped on to our problems. The problems that are there - we have to solve them, we have to think about them and work on them - but they are not everything. If you make it everything, then it will become everything. If you see only problems and nothing else then you will become more and more negative. We need to work on feeling positive, instead, which is about experiencing positive things.

*Instead of getting upset and
angry when you are hurt, you
can look at the situation and ask
yourself, 'What can I do to make
things better?'*

What to do when we feel hurt

Student: Once we have the desire to be happy and joyful in all situations, how would you advise us when people behave in a way that makes us feel upset or angry, even if we have done nothing wrong? What is the best way to deal with our own emotions so we can get back to a state of quilibrium?

Rinpoche: Two things are very important, I think. One is a deep understanding that if you react in a negative way, with upset and anger and that kind of thing, it does not help. It doesn't change the situation. You have a problem and want to change the situation: you want to be respected; you want to be loved, or something like that. If you just get angry or upset and cry, that doesn't make people respect you or love you. So, therefore, it is important to understand right from the beginning, very clearly, that that way of reacting does not produce good results. It does not even make you feel better, either. It is not helpful.

When you truly know this, you can say, 'Okay, some people respect me; some people don't respect me. Some people do good things; some people don't do good things.' Your life is full of all these problems or 'mistakes', these kinds of situations. You don't need to get too much upset by them. But we do need to do whatever will bring the best result out of the situation.

This is the second point. Instead of getting upset and angry and things like that, you can look at the situation and ask yourself, 'What can I do to make things better?' I think that is the best way to approach it. There are always different possibilities we can improve. When you are getting angry and upset and things like that, your way of looking at the situation - your attitude - is as if the story is finished: 'That is very bad!' like everything is all finished and done with. So you get angry and upset about it.

If you see, instead, that this is how the situation is right now, and ask yourself what way you could improve it, then you don't have to feel pessimistic or hopeless. You can feel optimistic. Things can be changed. I think this is an extremely important way of reacting. Of course, it is not easy. It does not happen just like that. We have our habitual tendencies. But we can still try to work on them and try to act in the best way.

Generating a sense of satisfaction and feeling rich in our heart is a matter of attitude and experience. We can develop and change our state of mind by learning how to feel contentment, how to feel good with what we have.

Inner generosity

Generosity covers two things. One is 'inner generosity'. Another is 'outer generosity'. Inner generosity means to work on your own poverty syndrome, the attitude of feeling 'I don't have, I lack,' always being needy: 'I need this. I need that. I don't have this. I don't have that.' Greedy; needy; a state of mind of always lacking something. And this is what it is - *a state of mind.*

Somebody can be very rich but still have this attitude. Nobody has enough. It is said that during Buddha's time there was an old lady who found a gold coin. It was a very nice, special gold coin and she thought she wanted to give it to somebody who really needed it. She asked Buddha who was the person who needed it the most. Buddha thought for a while and then he said that if she really wanted to give it to the person who needed it the most, she should give it to this particular man, who was actually the richest person in town.

The old lady was not very convinced but she was very devoted to Buddha so she went to this man and offered him the gold coin. She said, "I found this gold coin and I asked Buddha who I should give it to and he said you, but I am not convinced he is right."

And the man said, "He is absolutely right! Because I have 999 of the same gold coins and I am desperately looking for one more to make 1000!"

After 1000, he will want to make it 10,000. After 10,000, he will want to make it 100,000; then one million. And so on. This attitude of not having enough is not about having or not having. It is a habitual tendency. If you are not satisfied, you can have the whole world and still not be satisfied.

So we need to develop and change our state of mind by learning how to feel contentment, how to feel okay. It does not mean to say you should not have anything anymore or you should not improve on what you have. But you should feel good with what you have. So therefore, generating this sense of satisfaction and feeling rich in your heart, is a matter of attitude and experience.

I know this really well because I know a lot of rich people and I know a lot of poor people. It is not that poor people are actually poorer. Let me explain: In the predictions of all the spiritual traditions like Buddhism or Hinduism or others, they all seem to be saying that as time goes on, this is a degenerating time; that people are becoming poorer; life is becoming shorter, and things like that. And yet, from scientific record, it is going in the opposite direction. The lifespan of people is increasing. The wealth of people is increasing. So therefore, I was wondering which view is wrong. Then I think I came to understand it better. It is about the different ways of looking at whether you are rich or poor.

From the materialistic point of view, being rich means you have more money. You have a bigger bank balance. If you have two cars, then you are richer than if you have one. From the spiritual point of view, however, that is not the case. The more satisfied you are, the richer you are. It is not that if you have more, you are richer. You can have the whole world but, if you are not satisfied, then you are poor.

When we describe the hungry ghost realm, we talk about a type of hungry ghost who is guarding a treasure. It is said that this hungry ghost is guarding a big, big treasure and he is sitting in front of the door where everything is. He never leaves, not even for one second. He cannot enjoy anything of the treasure himself and he cannot allow anybody else to enjoy anything from the treasure. That is why he is a hungry ghost. Sometimes life is like that.

Generosity is a way to work on this kind of feeling - to learn to enjoy what you have, to appreciate what you have and also to learn how to share with one another. What we have and what we don't have is actually about how we feel, in the end.

Suffering is totally useless, and totally needless. If you can get rid of it, do so. No one needs suffering in order to get enlightened or to make more progress. If you are free of suffering, you are already free and have no problem.

Do we need suffering to progress?

Student: I was under the impression we need suffering in order to progress. Is this true? For example, when someone has got some form of suffering, is it that they need to have that experience in order to progress?

Rinpoche: That is not the Buddhist way of seeing it. The Buddhist way of understanding is that suffering is totally useless and totally needless. If you can get rid of it – no problem, get rid of it! You don't need it in order to get enlightened or in order to get anything. You don't need it to make more progress. It is totally unnecessary. That is the Buddhist way of seeing.

If you can get a little bit free of suffering, that is good. A little bit more, even better. More than that, better still. Because if you have no suffering, you don't *need* to progress - you are already completely progressed! This question often comes up. People think that a bit of suffering is necessary because it pushes you and inspires you to practice or get rid of suffering. But if you have no suffering, why do you need any inspiration to get rid of suffering? You are already free of suffering. So if you have no problem, why would you look for a problem to solve?

This is the Buddhist way of understanding. Maybe there are other cultural influences that would suggest something else, but from the Buddhist point of view there is nothing necessary about suffering. If we would *want* suffering, we would not need to do anything. We don't have to practice because Buddha or anyone else said we should. We do not do it because he said we had to get rid of suffering. We only need to get rid of suffering because we don't want suffering.

The whole question of suffering is this: Buddha saw that people were suffering. And he saw that they did not want to suffer; they really wanted to get rid of their suffering. So he thought, 'How to get free from suffering? - Is there a way or is there not a way?' He asked this, not because 'somebody high up' said something about it, but because everybody – me, you, everybody – do not want to have suffering. So Buddha investigated the question and tried many ways to find the answer. Eventually he found out that there is a way to be free from suffering - all different kinds of suffering and all different levels of suffering. All different levels of fear, actually; it is more like fear. But this freedom does not come from outside. It comes from within.

To get rid of everything that you don't want is very difficult. You might not want it to rain; you might not want it to be cold; you might not want it to be hot; you might not want that building there; you might not want this person here. Maybe today you don't like something but tomorrow you might like it. Tomorrow you like it but the day after tomorrow, maybe you won't like it again. To get rid of everything you don't want and to get hold of everything that you do want, is impossible. You cannot control everything and, even if you could, 'what you want' and 'what you do not want' changes all the time. There is no solution in this way.

Does that mean, therefore, I can never be free from suffering? Buddha said, 'Yes you can be free.' It is not that you can get rid of everything you don't want and get everything you do want, all the time. That is not possible. But you can do something from within yourself. You can change your way of reacting to things and change your way of looking at things. You can change your way of experiencing. If you can do that, you can have no more problems.

Certain situations in life are good to change, of course. Sometimes it is easier to change practical things than following another approach. There is one story, for example, about a great Hindu master who lived in Calcutta once, and who could walk on water on the River Ganges. Some of the college students there went to him and requested him to teach them how to walk on the water. They repeatedly asked him so that finally, he said to them, "See that boat on the river?"

"Yes," they said.

"See how easily it goes on top of the water?" He said.

"Yes."

"I think it is better to get a boat if you want to go on top of the water. It is much quicker and much easier than learning how to walk on water!" He told them it was more economical and easier, more beneficial, to learn how to row a boat than to learn how to walk on water. Even if you could learn how to walk on water, it would take so long to learn and then afterwards, if that is the only thing you can do, it may not be so useful. So maybe it is not the best way, not the best use of your time.

In the same way, of course we should change some things in life for the better, if we can. But eventually it is our way of reacting we need to work on. This is the way in which there is a real possibility to free ourselves. The problems will not necessarily all go away but how we look at them and how we react to them - how we experience our problems and our life - will be different. [iv]

*Meditation is more about relaxing,
being. So too much effort is not
useful. You are training through
being, not doing.
The mind has to liberate itself.
It has to find peace within itself.
It has to become flexible by itself.
This cannot happen in a forced way.*

Effort in Meditation

Student: Sometimes when I meditate my mind is like an energetic puppy who does not want to sit down. I make all this effort to try and get my mind to calm but then find that if I sit for a long time, my mind naturally quietens down, a bit like the puppy finally coming and sitting down of its own accord. So, I was wondering what the right balance is of making an effort in meditation and allowing something to arise by itself?

Rinpoche: Too much effort is actually not good, they say. It is more about relaxing, being. Too much effort is not useful. You are training through *being*, not through *doing*. So, you allow your mind to relax and be aware and learn how to let be. That is the best way of training. You *allow* your mind to rest. You don't *make* it 'sit' or anything. You don't force or push.

There are two ways of doing things generally. If someone pushes you and demands, 'You *must* sit down,' then you probably won't want to sit down. If they say, 'You can sit here if you like', then you might indeed feel like sitting there. If somebody says, 'Don't do this!' you are more likely to want to do it. That is what I am like, anyway.

Too much pressure, too much trying, does not work. If you are a bit more relaxed it will usually go much better. The mind has to liberate itself. It has to find peace within itself. It has to become flexible by itself. This cannot happen in a forced way. This is the approach of meditation. In shamatha [calm abiding] meditation you don't make lots of efforts. The skill is to let the mind be, so that naturally it becomes calmer. You relax and just maintain a little awareness.[iv]

When compassion and joy and positive deeds are increasing, that is the generation or accumulation of merit. But it is not really accumulating something; it is getting rid of something. It is getting rid of bad habits, negative actions and negative emotions.

Merit

We talk about two accumulations in Buddhism: the accumulation of merit and the accumulation of wisdom. The accumulation of wisdom is understanding and experiencing the way that things really are. The accumulation of merit is when our negative way of reacting and doing things decreases and positive actions increase. When compassion and joy and positive deeds are increasing, that is the accumulation of merit.

But merit is not something that you can accumulate like something you might put in a bag and then carry this heavy thing around. It does not really work like this. It is the same with what we call enlightenment, for instance. That result is described as *dral-thob* in Tibetan. It is 'the result that is attained by freeing,' by becoming *free from*. *Dral* is 'free from.'

If we become totally free from suffering and delusion, we become enlightened. It is not that we get something that we didn't have before. It is that we *get rid* of something – all the defilements, all the obstacles, all the obscurations - that prevented us from experiencing what we now experience. It is the result that comes from *uncovering* something, *getting rid* of something.

In the same way, accumulating merit is not really accumulating something. It is getting rid of something. It is getting rid of bad habits and negative actions and negative emotions. So, the accumulation is an accumulation of getting rid of something! [iv]

Vajrayana
Skilfull Means

Our true nature is that there is nothing fundamentally wrong. There is nothing much we need to add. Our true nature is free, and is already there. We just have to take off what is covering it.
When we truly realise this, then we become confident, because we know that there is absolutely nothing wrong at our core.

Our true nature

A very important aspect in getting rid of fear is to know that our true nature is that there is nothing wrong. There is nothing too much we need to put *on* or add. Our true nature is free, and is already there. We just have to take *off* what is covering it. When that becomes your idea or your way of seeing, then you become much more confident, because you know that there is absolutely nothing wrong at the core of you. Whatever is wrong is only something that has been kind of 'polluting' your true nature.

The Buddha gives the example of water. He said that water can be very polluted. It can have lots of dust and dirt and other things in it so that it becomes undrinkable. But even then it can be purified again, because the dirt is not the nature of the water. The nature of the water is pure. That is why it can be purified. It is the same with our true nature, which is our Buddhanature.

At the Mahayana or Bodhisattvayana level, our nature is there and it can be purified. In order to purify it we have to work on doing that; we have to get rid of these things that pollute it. That is how our nature is purified. That is the teaching. So we work on the Six Paramitas [which are Generosity, Morality, Patience, Diligence, Meditation and Wisdom] and that is how we practise.

The Vajrayana level, however, includes something more about Buddhanature. In the Vajrayana there is direct introduction to the nature of mind. This means that a person can be introduced directly to Buddhanature, the Buddhanature that is everybody's true nature. This needs the right kind of circumstances to happen. For example, the right kind of teacher can introduce somebody who is open enough to experience it. This is extremely important as a direct method of communicating called *transmission*. Transmission is a direct kind of teaching, which is not only about concepts. It uses a combination of conceptual and non-conceptual ways to communicate.

This is sometimes called introducing you to the nature of your mind.

In studies of Buddhist philosophy it is all about slowly leading us from concepts to non-concepts. The real true nature of the way things are is not conceptual. It is free from concepts. We need to go beyond concepts.

Truth and concepts

Words are like symbols, symbols of concepts. Words may mean totally different things for different people. But words are not the only things that we use when we communicate.

Generally when we communicate, even in our usual way, the words we use are only something like 20% of our communication. 80% of communication is through other ways, like the tone of our voice, our facial expression and other things like that. We use our hands, for example making gestures. Maybe our hands help? I don't know. At least sometimes a hand gesture might communicate that I don't know how to say what I want to say!

In the Vajrayana there is communication called direct introduction to the nature of mind. This is referred to as *transmission*. We talk about three methods of transmission: 'Mind to mind' transmission; Sign transmission; and 'Mouth to ear' transmission. Whichever way we are talking about, it is about *experiencing* our true nature *directly*.

That is what we call direct transmission of our true nature, referring to whatever means we realise this nature. It is not necessarily always a transmission given by another person. It is actually a discovery you make yourself. So, in the end, it cannot really be something given by somebody else. It means that you really, extremely clearly, see what your true nature is. You see what you are really all about. That is discovering Buddhanature.

This is something which is studied in the Bodhisattvayana and Vajrayana Buddhism. All the philosophies like Interdependence, Emptiness and Selflessness; all these teachings and discussions and analyses of the Mahayana or Bodhisattvayana are for studying Buddhanature. They are designed to lead to understanding our true nature. What we study in the literature is from a more intellectual angle. But these intellectual studies and reflections are a little bit different from common or usual studies.

In our usual studies we read something and then we can say, 'Yes, that's it. I have now understood it, finished. I've got it.' But in these studies of Buddhist philosophies and the like, it is all about slowly leading us from concepts to non-concepts. It is about taking us through reasoning and analysis to find out that whatever way we say it is, whatever way we grasp that things are, that is not actually the case. If you see it this way... that is not right. If you see it that way... that is not right. If you think you understand things to be this way... you find it is also not right. Whatever way we understand, it is not right, by which we mean it is not the whole or complete picture. So what can you do then?

The real true nature of the way things are is not conceptual. It is free from concepts. We need to go beyond concepts. We need to understand that the way things are is beyond any of the conceptual ways of grasping. That is the way it is. It is very difficult for our intellectual mind.

I don't know whether it happens to you or not, but when I studied Madhyamika [a main Buddhist philosophy], I almost went mad because of this! It is a very difficult subject to study, because there is nothing to grasp onto. Whatever you try to grasp at is cut off. You try and try...there must be something to grasp at... somewhere... But you find nothing that you can definitively hold on to. And that is the whole purpose. It leads you out into an almost meditative kind of a state.

It is neither this, nor that. It is beyond dogmas, beyond words, beyond grasping. It is beyond any ends. Sometimes we say it is beyond any extremes. 'Yes' is not right. 'No' is not right. 'Neither' is not right. 'Both' is not right. And then, if you want to reason further, you can subdivide into eight or 16 options, and none of them are right.

So you just have to experience it in the end - directly experience the way it is.

That's why the following story is so fantastic. I think it is a Christian story:

There was once this devil and his attendant and they were watching a human being walking up and down in the courtyard. The devil was watching the man, very intently. So the attendant was also looking at him very intently (because usually attendants do whatever the boss does!). Suddenly there was a big, shining explosion of light.

The attendant asked, "What happened? What happened?"

The devil said, kind of coolly, "Oh, he just found the truth."

The attendant was scared and asked, "That sounds very dangerous for us though - isn't it?" He had heard that truth was the downfall of the devil's kingdom.

The devil said, "No, it doesn't matter too much for us. Because the moment he tries to give it to someone else, the moment he tries to teach it to somebody else, that person will make it into a dogma. So there is no problem for us."

It is very difficult for us to go beyond dogmas. But that is the idea. The main thing, if we want to recognise our true nature, is that we have to go beyond concepts and dogmas and directly experience it. This is meditation, in a way, because it is a direct experience, that is not a grasping experience. It is not easy to talk about because, once we talk about something, it makes it a dogma, whatever we say. But experiencing the true nature of ourselves is very important and is the main thing in Vajrayana Buddhism.

When we can really experience our true nature, then we can completely relax in it. We can become completely fearless. We can find no reason why we should fear or have any of those negative emotions at all. We find the solution. We find the true fearlessness.

The main thing that drives us is not the conscious level; it is the unconscious level. Unless we can work at that deep level, we cannot change our way of perceiving, our way of experiencing and our way of reacting, completely.

Working at the experiential level

Finding true fearlessness is very difficult. Firstly, it is very difficult to go beyond concepts. Then it is also extremely difficult to transform the way I am - my habitual tendencies, my karma. We therefore need very direct methods to truly bring transformation. It cannot be done only through a conceptual way of working. For instance, just knowing intellectually 'I have to be more positive,' does not necessarily bring that change. We may know we have to become more positive but there is still the problem - how do we become more positive? Maybe we can start by looking for positive things to concentrate on. But there are often so many negative things going on, and so many problems, this is not enough alone.

This way of working is fine but it is only at the conceptual level. If we are consciously aware, it may work a bit at our conscious level. But what about the unconscious level? It does not work on that. And the main thing that drives us is not the conscious level; it is the unconscious level. Unless we can work at that deep level, we cannot change our way of perceiving, our way of experiencing and our way of reacting, completely. These come from deep down at a very deep level. This is where our emotions come from. Of course we can also work on our emotions consciously. We can say to ourselves, 'This is not good; this is not the way; this is not helping.' Slowly things can change a little bit through thinking like this. But it is difficult.

What is most important in the Vajrayana is to work on the way we are, not only at the conceptual level, but through working at the experiential level, the non-conceptual level. That is the main point. Usually it is said that the difference between the Vajrayana way of practising and the general way of practising is that the Vajrayana way uses the *result* as the path and the rest of the Buddha's teachings - the Sutrayana if you want to define it - uses the *cause* as the path.

What do we mean by that? For instance, if you want to generate compassion you need to generate positive experience, not negative. It is important because generally each of us does experience many problems, and our mind tends to focus on them.

The three most important things we need to work on developing are:

- Feeling positive, experiencing positive things
- Compassion
- Experiencing our true nature, which is wisdom

When we work on developing compassion, it opens our heart and we become more positive, also. So it is important to be kind to our self and to be kind to others. This is compassion. We also need to experience our positive side - happiness and joy. We need to talk and think about happiness, and feel happiness. And then, not only these, but we can experience our true nature, the truth, the way that we are. It is important to experience this also. The Vajrayana techniques are about working on these three aspects at a fundamental, or experiential, level.

We can use a Buddha or a Bodhisattva as the path. We start by visualising and feeling the presence of that kind of a being: someone who displays the greatest love, the greatest compassion, the greatest wisdom and the greatest power. As we visualise this presence, we are already practising feeling these qualities ourselves.

Using the result as the path

How do we work on feeling positive and compassion and experiencing our true nature – which is wisdom - from the Vajrayana perspective? The methods of the Vajrayana through which we work on these in a non-conceptual way, are called the *creation* and *completion* practices. There are many, many teachings on these and there are many, many slightly different practices given. But the core is very simple: it is a practice, by which we really mean it is a training. The practice in this Vajrayana way is called a *sadhana*. This is where we use the result as the path.

How could we use the result as the path? We could use a Buddha or a Bodhisattva as the path and that is the approach of a sadhana. For instance, we can take the example of Avalokiteshvara, the Bodhisattva or Buddha of Compassion (also called Chenrezig) or we could take the example of Tara, who is a female Bodhisattva and is said to be the Bodhisattva of Fearlessness. She is like an archetype of fearlessness, of courage.

What we do as the practice is to feel the presence of that kind of a Bodhisattva, for example a being of great fearlessness. We feel the presence of Tara in this way; we feel the energy of that kind of fearlessness. We feel the presence of not only Tara, but *all* the Enlightened Beings. We feel that energy, that presence.

We call this 'visualisation'. Sometimes people have problems with visualisation because they think they have to see something in particular. It is not so much about seeing; it is about *feeling*. It is feeling the presence of someone who displays the greatest love, the greatest compassion, the greatest wisdom and the greatest power. We could use the energy of anything in the whole universe that is like that.

If you can feel that presence, this is already a big practice because when you can feel the presence of somebody who is the embodiment of loving-kindness and compassion and enlightened wisdom, you are already practising the feeling of that. You are already practising compassion. You are practising wisdom. You are practising healing. And you are practising feeling good. It is a non-conceptual way of working on this, working directly.

Sometimes we say the Buddha is like an 'unacquainted friend'. He or she is somebody who we don't know, who we are not acquainted with, and yet they are our greatest friend. Someone who is always positive, always wanting to help, always trying to do something that will be helpful and bring positive benefit.

An un-acquainted friend

The main intention of all Buddhas and Bodhisattvas is to help all beings. And it is very important to understand that from the Buddhist point of view, when we talk about all the Buddhas and Bodhisattvas, we don't mean only *Buddhist* Buddhas and Bodhisattvas. When we say we feel the presence of all the Enlightened Beings, we mean it inclusively. The main intention of all these beings is to help and there is nothing called Buddhas or Bodhisattvas being angry with anybody.

Sometimes people say to me, 'Oh, I can't do this or that because then Buddha will be angry with me!'

This way of thinking is not in the Buddhist conceptual framework at all. Buddha cannot be angry with us. Even if he is angry, he cannot do anything wrong to us - so it would only be his misfortune! Nobody needs to be afraid of Buddha being angry. There is nothing like that from the Buddhist point of view. The Buddha is someone who is always positive, always wanting to help, always trying to help; always trying to do something that will be helpful and bring positive benefit.

So when we practice feeling the presence of a Buddha or a Bodhisattva, we feel the presence of somebody like that. Sometimes we say the Buddha is like an 'unacquainted friend'. He or she is somebody who we don't know, who we are not acquainted with, and yet they are our greatest friend. We feel the presence of a dear friend like that, who would never have any intention of doing anything that could affect us negatively in any way. All their intention is focussed on trying to help. Whatever we do, he or she will never feel badly towards us.

Not only that, but he or she is also full of wisdom, being completely wise and knowing everything. On top of that, he or she also has all the power needed to help and heal: full and complete healing power.

As I feel the presence of all the Buddhas and Bodhisattvas, I also feel the presence of all sentient beings, here with me, not excluding anyone. I embrace everyone, holding all sentient beings in my mind. When I feel together with every being in this way, I am working on compassion.

Everyone is included

When I am feeling the presence of a Buddha or Bodhisattva, together with all the Buddhas and Bodhisattvas around them, I am working on feeling positive qualities, through doing this. But that is not enough. I also feel the presence of all sentient beings here with me - my near and dear ones, my friends and acquaintances, anybody who I wish protection or healing for, and all beings existing throughout all of space. As I feel the presence of a fully-realised wise and compassionate Being, I feel all other beings are here with me too and are therefore also feeling this presence. Without leaving anybody out, I include everyone.

When I do that, what am I doing? I am embracing everyone in my mind. This is compassion. I am holding together all sentient beings in my mind. I am not excluding anyone. I cannot say, 'That person is ex-communicated. I am not talking to him. I am not including him.' Nobody is ex-communicated. Everybody is inside. I feel together with every being. When I feel together with every being in this way, I am working on compassion.

I am also working on fearlessness. Because, if I gather every being under my own arms, who would I fear? When I do this, what is happening? I want all beings to be freed, to be happy, to be healed, to be purified. So, therefore, I make a kind of request or prayer or wish or dedication or aspiration, or whatever you want to call it, that all these beings together with myself may be healed, purified and transformed. This is part of Vajrayana sadhana practice.

When I am making a wish or prayer or aspiration that all beings together with myself may be healed, purified and transformed; when I want to say that deeply, I can say it through a mantra.

Using a mantra

We use mantra in the Vajrayana as a way of making a kind of request or prayer; as a way of voicing a wish or aspiration. A mantra is a kind of prayer. When I say a mantra, while I am visualising a Buddha or Bodhisattva, then I feel that healing energy from this Being or their mandala or all the Buddhas and Bodhisattvas and all their positive energy, radiates light or a kind of healing power. I *feel* as if this is happening and this creates the possibility for the practice to be a physical experience.

I feel the light or radiance - or sometimes it is a flow of nectar or something like that - I feel it in my body. I feel the warmth of it, the cleansing power of it. It may bring some kind of bliss or joy, receiving that. I feel that my body is completely purified and all that is negative in my body and mind is purified. The negative karma, negative emotions, pain and problems, whatever negativity is there, it is all purified. I feel the joy of being purified.

I not only feel the joy for myself but I feel that every being is purified and every being is feeling the same way. When I am feeling like that, what is happening to me is that I am actually working on my compassion because I am allowing this to happen to all sentient beings without exception. And I am working on feeling positive because when I am feeling that everybody has been purified and healed and transformed, who is feeling that? I am feeling that.

When I feel that everybody is in that totally purified, totally transformed state of mind, totally healed state of being, I cannot feel otherwise – I have to feel joyful, I have to feel happy! If I really feel that everybody is happy and joyful, it is not possible that a smile does not come across my face, involuntarily. So, therefore, I am working on being happy, in a way, and being fearless. That is the practice, just doing it: Not intellectually thinking, 'I have to feel like this, I have to do this', but just feeling it and experiencing it directly.

Then, at the end of a visualisation the Being, for instance Tara, dissolves into light and dissolves into me. I feel that the Tara and myself are inseparable. Because my true nature and Tara's true nature is exactly the same. It is no different. Our true nature and the Buddha's true nature is no different; it is exactly the same way. Therefore, I feel exactly the same as the Tara. I can let my mind be totally relaxed and fearless, as Tara might be. When I can relax like that, in an uncontrived way - not thinking of the past, not thinking of the future, not manipulating the present, just being completely natural - actually that is experiencing the real nature of our mind. So, therefore, that is the practice of wisdom.

The teacher – student relationship is the learning process in the Vajrayana. It is the means by which a student can learn to practise correctly and sincerely and deeply.

The teacher - student relationship

In the Vajrayana, much emphasis is placed upon the teacher-student relationship. This relationship is the learning process. It is nothing else but learning how to practice correctly, and how to do so sincerely and deeply.

The relationship doesn't mean you receive a gift. That would be to miss the point. You need to really understand how to do the practice. That is why it is said that the more you practice and the better your practice is, the more your devotion to the teacher grows. Your devotion increases when you experience the good effects, the beneficial results of the practice. The more you feel the healing result of the practice, the more your confidence in the teachings grows. The more your confidence in the teachings grows, the stronger your confidence in your teacher becomes.

That is why Milarepa told Gampopa, his best student, 'I have given you all the teachings, now go away to central Tibet and practice there. One day it will so happen that you will see your old teacher, me, as a real Buddha. That is the time you can start teaching, because then you will have really got it, then you will have really understood.'

I think this carries a strong message, because if you really understand and really benefit and come to deal with problems through your practice, then your confidence, faith and trust in the teachings and the teacher increases. This is the reason why, from the Tibetan Buddhist point of view, the more devotion you have for your teacher, the more you know you have truly benefited from the teachings. ᵛ

Tara, An Example

The practice of Tara takes her as an inspiration to work on bringing fearlessness to ourselves and eventually to all beings: freeing all beings from fear and pain and suffering. The practice is to awaken our own latent qualities of wisdom and compassion, which are ultimately the same as Tara's.

Tara

Buddha talked about the concept of 'Tara,' and sometimes it is said that Tara was the first and most basic kind of tantra that Buddha taught. He told the story of a young princess who lived a long, long time ago, during the time of another Buddha – Buddha Amoghasiddhi. This princess was very compassionate and courageous. She made an aspiration, or decision, to work to benefit all beings, especially to free them from their fears: to save all beings from all kinds of fear and danger and suffering. She went to the Buddha of that time and made the promise that she would not only dedicate this life, but also all her lives to come, to bringing lasting peace and happiness and, especially, to protect people from any kind of fear and danger. Thus she became what we call a Bodhisattva.

She made an additional special promise to herself that, in all her lifetimes, she would never be born a man; she would always be female. She vowed that, throughout her Bodhisattvahood and even after Buddhahood, she would always take the female form. Only through the female form would she be working for the benefit of all beings. When she made this strong and special kind of a promise, it is said that all the Buddhas and Bodhisattvas rejoiced in the promise she had made. They very much praised her for her dedication and special kind of commitment.

Since that time, Tara not only became a Bodhisattva, but also fully enlightened. But she had made the promise that she would not become enlightened until everybody has become enlightened, so she does not want to be called a Buddha. She is a Buddha but she doesn't like it if you call her a Buddha. She prefers to be called a Bodhisattva.

Because she has been helping people for such a long time, it is said that there is actually no Buddha now, who has not been helped by her and through her help came to Buddhahood. Therefore, she is sometimes called the Mother of all the Buddhas. She has been, in one way or another, involved in helping all Buddhas to become Buddhas. As a result, many, many great masters use Tara as their main practice; as an aspiration, as an inspiration, as a model and also to call on for help.

It is said that generally the feminine aspects of life are swifter to act, to help – in the same way as the mother is often quicker to come when her child cries, than the father. It is usually understood in this tradition, and maybe in others also, that whenever there is a feminine Bodhisattva or Buddha or energy, the action or response will be swifter. It is said that if you pray to Tara, things will happen more quickly, whereas if you pray to Buddha they may take longer.

When we talk about the practice of Tara we mean taking this inspiration as a model. It does not mean it is only for women to practice. It means it is a method to work on bringing fearlessness to yourself and others and to free you from all kinds of suffering and pain and problems - and to do so quickly. Eventually it is to bring lasting peace and happiness to all beings, as much as possible, and as quickly as possible. According to the legend of Tara, she would help 100,000 beings before she would even have her breakfast! Then she would help 100,000 beings after breakfast also. So she was working very hard, and very quickly, with very responsive action.

There are many different Taras: White Tara, Green Tara, Yellow Tara, Blue Tara, Red Tara, 21 Taras, 108 Taras, Eight Taras; all different kinds of emanations with slightly different energies. But the main practice of Tara is that you try to bring the quality of Tara, that kind of energy – the wisdom of Tara, the compassion of Tara – you bring it in yourself. You awaken that Tara aspect of your own nature.

From the Buddhist point of view, everybody has Buddhanature. The way we are, the way everybody is, and the way Tara is, is essentially exactly the same. It is just that we have not been able to be awakened to that latent quality that we have. We need to awaken ourselves to that. We need to bring that out. We need to recognise it and awaken the qualities of wisdom and compassion within ourselves. If we can do that, then we have 'realised Tara.' We have become enlightened as Tara. That is the understanding of practising Tara. [iv]

White Tara holds the stem of an Utpala flower at her heart. Such a flower remains untouched by pollution and looks fresh all the time, even if it grows where there is a lot of dirt and mud. This is like wisdom: even if there are lots of problems and negativity, these cannot touch wisdom, because wisdom is knowing the true nature of things.

The imagery of White Tara

Out of all the different emanations of Tara, White Tara is especially called upon for accomplishment of whatever your wishes are for auspiciousness, for long life and for healing. White Tara is supposed to be extremely powerful for healing and for long life, including bringing freedom from all kinds of maladies and poverty and any kind of downfalls that would prevent these. This is what she is usually called on for.

White Tara has seven eyes, which symbolise that she sees all the 'Seven Worlds', meaning that she sees everything. The gesture or mudra her right hand is in is called the Giving mudra or Generosity mudra. This signifies she gives protection and freedom from suffering through bringing whatever people wish for.

Her left hand is in the mudra of the Three Jewels - Buddha, Dharma and Sangha - and holds the stem of a flower called an Utpala flower. This flower usually symbolises wisdom, like a lotus flower does. Even if these kinds of flowers are growing in very dirty places where there is a lot of dust and dirt and mud, the flower itself looks untouched by all of that. It is unstained and untouched by the pollution and looks fresh all the time. This is like wisdom: even if there are lots of problems and negativity, these cannot touch wisdom, because wisdom is knowing the true nature of things.

Therefore, the flower symbolises wisdom and the gesture of giving symbolises compassion. Usually there are three flowers. One is a bud, not yet open; one is in full blossom; and the last is over or finished. These signify that Tara is working for the three times - the past, the present and the future – all the time, with wisdom and compassion.

She is wearing the dress of a princess, not a monk or nun, not an ascetic. She wears all the finery and adornments of a princess to symbolise that there is nothing more to give up. She has accomplished everything. There is nothing left to purify or get rid of. All the qualities are accomplished. All the positive qualities of wisdom and compassion are fully realised. There is nothing left to wash off or get rid of or work on. She is sitting on a lotus flower and a moon disc. The lotus flower always signifies being free from samsara, being in the enlightened state.[iv]

Suffering is an experience, an individual experience, which arises when we react to whatever is happening with confusion or aversion or dissatisfaction. Therefore, if I am trying to help get rid of suffering, it has to be done individually. But many people can still work on this at the same time and be helped alongside each other.

Meeting suffering

Student: My question is about how we can live with the knowledge of the immensity of suffering that is everywhere. We can each do our best to 'do our bit' and help where we can. But it sounds like Tara committed to addressing the immensity of the suffering, forever. I am trying to understand what was involved in Tara making such a commitment, to meet the suffering wherever she went and help in whatever way she could.

Should we understand, for example, that when Tara helps people, she works specifically and individually with each case of suffering that she meets? And there isn't any short cut to address all the suffering at once? The suffering of this world seems to be so perpetual and so widespread, but should we still understand that the aim is to work with each incident and each individual case of suffering as we meet them?

Rinpoche: In order to help people become free from suffering, is it necessary to work with each and every individual, or is there a way to do something so that everybody is freed from suffering altogether?

The question we need to ask first is: What is suffering? Is suffering something that is somewhere 'out there', as if it is hanging in the air or existing in a way like that? No, it is nothing like that. Suffering is an experience, an individual experience. And that individual experience of suffering arises when I react to whatever is happening with confusion or aversion or dissatisfaction. The way we experience defines whether there is suffering or not. Therefore, from the Buddhist way of seeing things, if I need to get rid of suffering, the solution is not going to come from changing things 'out there.'

If the weather is good, for example, it does not necessarily mean the end of suffering. Maybe it helps a little bit but it does not bring the end of suffering. If everything is green and beautiful, that does not bring the end of suffering. The end of suffering has to be due to myself – how I experience, how I react to things, how I look at things, how I deal with my thoughts and emotions and perceptions and feelings.

If I am trying to help get rid of this suffering, it therefore has to be done individually. At any one time, there can be many people together, for example in one room. And someone can be suffering more than the others. Someone can be suffering less than the others. Some people there may not be suffering at all. Suffering is not something that is either existing or not existing in the room. It is due to how each individual reacts and experiences. Because it is like this, we can't all together be made free from suffering at once. That would be very difficult.

In the story of Tara it says that she freed 100,000 people from suffering before breakfast. That is a lot of individuals! I don't know if it happened exactly like the story. That is the legend. But what I think it means to show is that becoming free from suffering is not something that many people cannot do at once, alongside each other. It is not that, 'Now I am doing it. It is not your turn, so you cannot do it. You have to wait till I have finished.' It is not like that. Many people can still work on becoming free from suffering at the same time, and be helped alongside each other. But suffering and becoming free from suffering is a case of individual experience. That is the idea. [iv]

The point of meditation is not about getting a nice experience. The real purpose of meditation is learning how to deal with any kind of experience. How you react to what you experience is what is important. That is what meditation is about.

The true purpose of meditation

When we talk about the practice of meditation, I think it is very important to understand what the result of meditation is supposed to be. Sometimes people say, 'Oh, my meditation is going so well. It is so nice, so calm. It is so nice because there are no thoughts coming. It is very good.' Then they come the next day saying, 'Ah no, I have lost that. Where has it gone? I want it back.' Or 'I had such a nice experience last weekend when I went on a retreat. Now I can't get it back.'

The point of meditation is not about getting a nice experience. A nice experience sometimes happens but a nice experience never stays like that all the time. Sometimes a nice experience comes; sometimes a not-so-nice experience comes. To get a nice experience is not the purpose we engage in meditation for.

What is the real purpose of doing meditation then? The real purpose of meditation is learning how to deal with any kind of experience. That is why it is said that when you have a good experience and you go to your teacher and you say, 'Ah, I am having such a nice experience!' The teacher will say, 'It's okay, but it doesn't matter so much. It is neither so good nor so bad.' Then when you come and say, 'Ah, I am having a terrible experience!' He or she will say, 'It is nothing so bad - nothing so good, nothing so bad. It doesn't matter so much.'

It is not about what you experience. That is not important. How you react to what you experience is what is important. That is what meditation is about. If you only want a nice experience, you don't have to meditate. You could eat ice cream instead, or have a chocolate. I think that would work better than meditating. Why meditate for half an hour? Just have a chocolate! If you only want to have a nice experience.

The reason we meditate is not about having a nice experience. It is about learning to deal with our experience. If I learn how to deal with any experience, I can let it come and let it go. If a good experience comes, I can let it come and let it go. If a bad experience comes, I can let it come and let it go. Then I have meditation. And that is how to deal with problems and suffering, also. [iv]

Formal meditation practice is a training, but the real practice is wisdom and compassion. The real practice is that your mind becomes clear, aware, mindful and compassionate. The point is to bring the quality of calmness, clarity and awareness we experience in our meditation into our lives, because this is what is needed in life.

The real practice

Student: I practise the sadhana of White Tara quite regularly but sometimes it feels as if I have left my practice behind when I close the shrine room door. I wonder if you could say something about integrating the qualities of Tara that we might experience sitting on a cushion in a shrine room; integrating them with our lives, looking after small children for example.

Rinpoche: Vajrayana practice is inclusive of all the teachings of the Sravakayana and Mahayana or Bodhisattvayana. Everything that is presented in those vehicles is there, also, in the Vajrayana. And then on top of that we have 'creation' and 'completion' practices, or 'generation' and 'completion'. Creation practice is when you visualise the deity and is basically shamatha practice: a way to meditate and make your mind calm and clear.

The creation phase also has an extra skilful means contained within it. Usually when you meditate, you can meditate on your breathing or something like that as a focus for your mind, so you are not distracted or taken away from the meditation. We can use any kind of a focus for this. But when we use a deity as our focus, as we do in Vajrayana practice, we are not only using a focus to maintain that stability of our mind but we are also working on our habitual tendencies.

Our habitual tendencies are that we have a very strong identification with things – with our past, with our future: 'I am like this,' 'I am like that.' When you visualise yourself as Tara, or any other deity, your mind is focused on a being who is free from negative emotions, who expresses fully-enlightened wisdom and compassion. So, therefore, you are doing two things at once: maintaining stability and calmness of mind and also creating the habitual tendency to focus on something completely pure. That is the creation phase.

Also within the formal practice, you have the completion phase, the purpose of which is to understand the nature of the mind and the nature of reality.

Altogether this is the formal practice of Tara. But what is the *real* practice? The real practice is wisdom and compassion. The real practice is that your mind becomes clear, aware, mindful and compassionate. So when you are within the session of formal practice, you concentrate on the practice wholeheartedly. When you have finished your session, it is not that you have to see yourself as Tara the whole time necessarily, but the point is that you bring that quality of calmness, clarity and awareness into your life. You do not do it because you are 'doing Buddhist practice.' You do it because it is necessary to do this to get through life.

Whenever you are agitated or feeling negative you can say, 'This is useless, I should not focus in this way. I know it is neither good for me nor good for anybody else. If I don't do this it will be better for everybody.' And you try to focus on something more positive. Similarly, if I find my mind is disturbed by too many thoughts, then also I can say, 'This is not the way to go about life.' And this is when we can fall back on the experience we have had during meditation. We try to recall the experience we had during meditation and relax in it. It doesn't mean that we suddenly have to go away and meditate for a while. It is something we just quietly do within ourselves.

If you can bring these things into your life, even a little bit, then I think that is good practice. In some ways, this is better practice than doing lots of mantras in your shrine room. This is the real practice. I always see it that when you are doing the formal practices – whether it is the Tara sadhana or any type of meditation or retreat – I see this as a training for practice. The training is not the real practice. The real practice is life; how you actually deal with life, your problems and emotions. That is where the true practice is. If you have some training to help you practice, maybe it can help you in your daily life. If it does not help in your life, then the training was not very good. That would be a useless kind of training. I think it is very important to understand this.[iv]

Buddhas cannot wash away your negativity with water.
They cannot take away your suffering with their hands.
They cannot pour their realisation directly into you.
Only by showing the true nature of things, can they bring liberation.

Translated from the sutras of the Buddha

Dedication

All my babbling,
In the name of Dharma
Has been set down faithfully
By my dear students of pure vision.

I pray that at least a fraction of the wisdom
Of those enlightened teachers
Who tirelessly trained me
Shines through this mass of incoherence.

May the sincere efforts of all those
Who have worked tirelessly
Result in spreading the true meaning of Dharma
To all who are inspired to know.

May this help dispel the darkness of ignorance
In the minds of all living beings
And lead them to complete realisation
Free from all fear.

Ringu Tulku

Glossary and Notes

Amoghasiddhi (*don yod grub pa* Tibetan) is the Buddha of the Karma family. His name means 'the accomplishment of what is meaningful.'

Avalokiteshvara (also called **Chenrezig**) (*spyan ras gzigs* Tibetan) is the Bodhisattva of Compassion, an emanation of the Buddha Amitabha. He is the compassionate aspect of the mind of the Buddhas manifesting in the form of a deity, and is revered as the patron deity of Tibet. The most common forms in which he appears are the four-armed and the 1000-armed Chenrezig.

Bodhicharyavatara is a classic Mahayana or Bodhisattvayana text, which describes the path of the Bodhisattva. It was written by Shantideva, a great Indian scholar, who composed it while seemingly an ordinary monk at the great Nalanda Monastery. It was composed sometime in the 8th century, found wide acclaim almost immediately in India and was translated into Tibetan during the 9th century.

Bodhicitta (*Bodhichitta* Sanskrit; *byang chub kyi sems* Tibetan) is the heart essence of the Buddha, of enlightenment. The root of the word, *Bodh*, means 'to know', to have the full understanding' and *citta* refers to the heart-mind or 'heart feeling'. In a practical sense, Bodhicitta is compassion imbued with wisdom.

Bodhisattva (Sanskrit; *changchub sempa* Tibetan) comes from the root *bodh* which means to know, to have the full understanding. The term describes a being who has made a commitment to work for the benefit of others to bring them to a state of lasting peace and happiness and freedom from all suffering. A Bodhisattva does not have to be a Buddhist but can come from any spiritual tradition or none. The key thing is that they have this compassionate wish to free all beings from suffering, informed by the wisdom of knowing this freedom is possible.

Bodhisattvayana is the same as the **Mahayana** (literally 'Great Vehicle') of Buddhism, and is the path of the Bodhisattva. It emphasises the Buddha's teachings on interdependence, compassion and Bodhicitta. This expands on the teachings of the Sravakayana (the foundational vehicle of Buddhism), seeing the purpose of enlightenment as being the liberation of all sentient beings from suffering, as well as oneself. The vow of the Bodhisattva is to work towards bringing all beings to freedom from suffering. See also *Sravakayana, Mahayana*.

Buddhadharma is the teachings of the Buddha. It refers to the entire body of oral and written Buddhist teachings, and includes the literal teachings and that which is learnt through practising them.

Buddhanature / Buddha nature (*Sugatagarba* Sanskrit; *bde gshegs snying po* Tibetan) refers to the fundamental, true nature of all beings, free from any obscuration or distortion. Ultimately, our true nature and the true nature of all beings is inseparable from the nature of Buddha. This is the 'primordial goodness' of sentient beings, an innate all-pervasive primordial purity.

Chenrezig, see *Avalokiteshvara*.

Completion stage, in Vajrayana practice, is the stage of practice when the visualisation generated by the creation stage (see below) is dissolved, back into the mind of the practitioner, from whence it came. The practitioner then has a chance to rest in the non-dual reality pointed towards by the practice.

Creation stage, in Vajrayana practice, is the process by which a practitioner visualises and feels the presence of a deity or embodiment of enlightened energy. It refers to the general and specific generation of this feeling and view, and trains the mind of the practitioner in many ways, for example familiarising them with calm and one-pointed concentration.

Deity / Deities (*istadevata* Sanskrit; *yi-dam* Tibetan) in Buddhism, are representations of the embodiment of enlightened mind. They are visualised or depicted in various forms to bring out different aspects of its essential purity. During formal practice a practitioner may visualise a deity in front of, or above themselves, or as themselves. Deities encourage us to see the pure state of reality, by which we mean the state that does not bind us or create problems and is, therefore, a liberating state.

Dharma (Sanskrit; *chö* Tibetan) The word dharma has many uses. In its widest sense it means all that can be known, or the way things are. The other main meaning is the teachings of the Buddha; also called the *Buddhadharma*. See *Buddhadharma*.

Dilgo Khyentse Rinpoche (1910 - 1991) was an outstanding Dzogchen master and lineage holder of the Nyingma School of Tibetan Buddhism. He was a root teacher of Ringu Tulku.

Eightfold Path (or **Noble Eightfold Path**) describes eight aspects of 'the path of noble beings': Right or 'perfect' View, Thought, Speech, Action, Livelihood, Effort, Mindfulness and Concentration. The path of practice is the cultivation and development of these.

Emptiness (*shunyata* Sanskrit; *tong pa nyi* Tibetan) The Buddha taught, in the second turning of the wheel of Dharma, that all phenomena have no real, independent existence of their own. Things only appear to exist as separate, nameable entities because of the way we commonly, conceptually, see them. But in themselves, all things are 'empty' of inherent existence. Everything exists in an interdependent way. Ringu Tulku says in *Like Dreams and Clouds*: 'Emptiness does not mean there is nothing; emptiness means the way everything is, the way everything magically manifests'.

Gampopa (1079 – 1153) was the foremost disciple of Milarepa. He was a skilled physician and family man until an epidemic took the lives of his wife and children, at which point he became a monk and dedicated his life to Dharma. He received teachings from many sources and brought together earlier streams of Kadampa and Mahamudra teaching lineages to form the Kagyu school. He had many students, among them Düsum Khyenpa who became the first Karmapa. Gampopa wrote *The Jewel Ornament of Liberation* which is now a seminal Kagyu text.

Generation stage, see *Creation stage.*

Habitual tendencies (*she ki drib pa* Tibetan) Literally translated from Tibetan as 'obscurations of knowledge,' these refer to our propensity to act or react in certain ways, reinforced and influenced by past actions. They become ingrained in us again and again until they are habitual.

Hungry ghosts exist in a realm where they can never find satisfaction. They represent insatiable craving and are portrayed as having very small mouths and thin necks but large bellies.

Interdependence describes a fundamental Buddhist philosophy or view. It may also be called Dependent Origination, Interdependent Origination, Co-dependent Arising, Co-dependent Origination or Emptiness. All phenomena are understood as existing, not as discrete entities, but arising due to myriad interdependent conditions. See *Emptiness*.

Jataka Tales are stories about the previous lives of the Buddha, in both human and animal form, from about the 4th century BC. The being that was to become the Buddha appears in these tales in many forms, for example, a king, an outcast, a god or an elephant; but always exhibiting a virtue brought out by the tale.

Kagyu (Tibetan) *Ka* means 'oral' and *gyu* means 'lineage': the lineage of oral transmission. Also known as the 'Lineage of Meaning and Blessing' or the 'Practice Lineage'. One of the four major schools of Buddhism in Tibet, it was founded in Tibet by Marpa and is headed by His Holiness the Karmapa, currently HH 17th Karmapa Urgyen Trinley Dorje. The other three main schools of Tibetan Buddhism are the Nyingma, Sakya and Gelug.

Karma (Sanskrit; *lay* Tibetan) literally means 'action.' It refers to the cycle of cause and effect that is set up through our actions. Actions coloured or motivated by *klesha* (see below), for example anger or desire, will tend to create results in keeping with them and increase our tendency to do similar actions. These tendencies become ingrained in us and become our habitual way of being, which is our karma. According to our level of awareness, we can change our karma through consciously refining our actions.

Karmapa is the name of a series of great lamas of the Kagyu school, whose lineage of reincarnations goes back to Dusum Khyenpa (1110 – 1193). They were the first tulkus recognised in Tibet. See also *Kagyu*.

Klesha (*kleśa* Sanskrit; *nyön mong* Tibetan) refer to the mental defilements, mind poisons or negative emotions. They include any emotion or mind state that disturbs or distorts consciousness. They bring forth our experience of suffering and prevent our experience of love, joy and happiness. The three main kleshas are attachment (or desire), aversion (or anger) and ignorance. Combinations of these give rise to the five kleshas, which are these three plus pride and jealousy.

Lama (Tibetan; *guru* Sanskrit) means teacher or master. *La* refers to there being nobody higher in terms of spiritual accomplishment and *ma* refers to compassion like a mother. Thus both wisdom and compassion are brought to fruition together in the Lama.

Madhyamika (Sanskrit) literally means 'The Middle Way' and is the most influential of four major philosophical schools of Indian Buddhism. It is the Middle Way which avoids falling into the extremes of either eternalism or nihilism.

Mahayana Buddhism (*Mahayana* Sanskrit; *tek pa chen po* Tibetan) translates as 'Great Vehicle.' This is the second vehicle of Buddhism, which emphasises the teachings on interdependence, compassion and Bodhicitta. It expands on the teachings of the Sravakayana (the foundational vehicle of Buddhism) and sees the purpose of enlightenment as being the liberation of all sentient beings from suffering, as well as oneself. This is the path of the Bodhisattva (see above) and so may also be called the Bodhisattvayana. See also *Bodhisattvayana*.

Mandala (Sanskrit; *kyil khor* Tibetan) meaning a circle, having a centre and an edge, it literally refers to everything that exists within the periphery of the circle. In Buddhism, the mandala of a teacher refers to everything and everyone associated with that person. Mandala can also refer to an actual or graphic representation that symbolises all aspects of a deity and acts as a support for meditation. It can also be a symbolic representation of the entire universe, which can be visualised and offered in its purest form for the benefit of all beings.

Mantra (Sanskrit; *sngags* Tibetan) The word mantra is an abbreviation of two syllables mana and tara, respectively meaning 'mind' and 'protection': coming from the mind, giving protection through transformation. Mantras are Sanskrit words or syllables that express the quintessence of particular energies or of a deity. They protect the mind from distraction and serve as support for meditation. Mantras can be sung or spoken out loud, quietly recited 'just loud enough for your collar to hear' or recited silently.

Milarepa (1040 – 1123) is perhaps the most famous and well-loved Tibetan poet-saint. He was the quintessential wandering yogi, famous for his spontaneous songs of realisation. After an inauspicious early career as a black magician, he is said to have attained complete enlightenment in one lifetime through the arduous trials and teachings of his guru, Marpa the Translator. Gampopa became his spiritual heir.

Mudra is a Sanskrit word that means 'seal'. A mudra is a gesture, for example made with the hands during ritual practice alongside visualisation, to embody the feeling of, for example making an offering or similar. Deities display various mudras to signify different aspects, for example teaching the Dharma or giving / generosity.

Paramita / Six Paramitas or *'perfections'* lay out the path of practice for a Bodhisattva. They start with Generosity, which is paramount for the Bodhisattva, whose main motivation is compassion. They unfold, one from the other, Wisdom informing them all, bringing them to the transcendental level of *Paramita*, untainted by attachment and other negative mind states. The Six Paramitas are Generosity, Morality (Ethics or Good Conduct), Patience, Diligence, Meditation and Wisdom.

Patrul Rinpoche (1808 - 1887) was an outstanding master of Tibetan Buddhism of the 19th century. He was a great scholar and Dzogchen master who wrote the *Words of My Perfect Teacher*, a classic for the Nyingma school. Some of the most important living Dzogchen and Mahamudra lineage teachings today, came from Patrul Rinpoche.

Sadhana (*sgrub thabs* Tibetan), literally 'means of accomplishment,' refers to the text of a ritual practice that may be followed by a practitioner who has been initiated into it. A typical sadhana structure usually starts with taking refuge and arousing Bodhicitta. The main part of the practice involves visualisation and mantra recitation and the sadhana concludes by dedicating the merit of the practice to all sentient beings.

Samsara / samsaric (Sanskrit; *kor wa* Tibetan) is the state of suffering of 'cyclical existence'. It describes a state of mind that experiences gross and / or subtle pain and dissatisfaction. It arises because the mind is deluded and unclear and thus perpetually conditioned by attachment, aversion and ignorance.

Sangha consists of beings who have experience of the Dharma. It may be one person or a group of people. Buddha is the highest Sangha, because he has the highest realisation of Dharma.

Shamatha (Sanskrit; *zhi gnas* Tibetan) or **Shiné** is calm abiding meditation: calming and stabilising the mind to bring it to a state of peace. Sometimes also called tranquillity meditation.

Sravakayana (Sanskrit), 'the vehicle of the hearers and listeners', follows the common teachings of the Buddha which form the foundation of all Buddhist vehicles. The Sravakayana covers the commonly used term Hinayana (or 'small vehicle') as well as the Pratyekabuddhayana (or 'solitary realisers'). The emphasis of these paths is on personal liberation from the suffering of samsara.

Sutra / sutras (*mdo* Tibetan) are the teachings given by Shakyamuni Buddha, memorised by his disciples and subsequently written down.

Sutrayana is one of the divisions of practice made in Indo-Tibetan Buddhism. It follows the teachings and practices based on the sutras (see above). The other division in this system is the Tantrayana, which follows the teachings based on the tantras. The Sutrayana is sometimes considered the 'causal' vehicle because the path that is followed establishes the causes of enlightenment. See also *Tantrayana*.

Tantra (Sanskrit; *gyu* Tibetan) literally means 'continuity' or continuous thread (of the pure nature of mind) that runs through everything. In Buddhism, it also refers to the meditative practices of the Vajrayana, which include mantra recitation and visualisation, and the texts that describe these.

Tantrayana is the vehicle that follows the teachings of the tantras. It is synonymous with the Vajrayana or Mantrayana. It takes the result of enlightenment, the true nature of mind, as its path and so is sometimes referred to as the 'result' vehicle. See also *Vajrayana, Sutrayana*.

Three Jewels refer to **Buddha** (as the expression of ultimate nature), **Dharma** (the teachings and therefore path to the freedom of realizing this ultimate nature) and **Sangha** (the ideal spiritual community, which understands and can therefore support this path). These three are regarded as the perfect objects in which to seek refuge from the unsatisfactory nature of cyclical existence, or samsara.

Transmission is direct teaching of the true nature of things, which goes beyond a purely conceptual understanding. It may use a combination of conceptual and non-conceptual means to communicate. Three means of transmission are referred to: 'Mouth to ear,' 'Sign' and 'Mind to mind.' By these means, lineages of realisation are established and maintained.

Tulku is the title given to someone who has been recognized as the rebirth (re-incarnation) of a previous realised master or lama.

Utpala flower rises from mud and is like the water lily or lotus, a symbol of purity and wisdom.

Vajrayana Buddhism (Sanskrit; *dorje tek pa* Tibetan) *Vajra* means 'diamond-like' or of 'indestructible capacity,' conveying a sense of what is beyond arising and ceasing and is therefore indestructible; the indestructible nature of wisdom that sees through illusion. The Vajrayana is the third vehicle of Buddhism and incorporates and accepts all the teachings of the Sravakayana and the Bodhisattvayana (or Mahayana). Vajrayana then also includes teachings on the tantras and various skilful means. It is the method of taking the result as the path and may afford the practitioner swift progress, practised in accordance with the foundations of Buddhist approach. See also *Mahayana, Sravakayana*.

Editor's Note: Throughout the Heart Wisdom series we have used the word *student* to identify questions and discussion from audience members. This is not intended to imply the speaker would necessarily identify themselves as a student of Tibetan Buddhism or of Ringu Tulku. It refers to how they are being a 'student' in this instance, by asking a question in order to understand more.

Source Notes

i   Public talk: *'The intelligent heart – creating happiness in our lives.'* Oxford, June 2012.

ii Public talk: *'Meditation.'* London, May 2009.

iii Bodhicharyavatara Online Shedra course Teaching BA4_21-27: *The sufferings of samsara and the need to seize the opportunity.* Dec 2011.

iv Question and answer discussion with White Tara group, Oxford 2012.

v   Teaching: *'How to transform emotions into wisdom'* Samye Dzong, Barcelona, Nov 1997.

Acknowledgments

As with any, even small book, many have contributed to this volume. From the students who organised the talks and seminars and group discussions at which these teachings were given, through to the proof-readers and publications team who helped with the final product. Thank you to everyone who has collectively brought this book to fruition.

Thank you to Margaret Ford who set up the publications team and the Heart Wisdom series. Thank you to the White Tara Group in Oxford for all our gatherings and discussions, which informed the format of this book. Thank you to Anna Howard for organising this group and offering comment on this book and the preface. Thank you to Jonathan Clewley for proof-reading the text at an early stage and offering helpful comments and suggestions. Thank you to Cait Collins for the quote from the Lazy Lama series and to Mariette van Lieshout for proof reading the final draft.

Thank you to Rachel Moffitt for invaluable administrative support on the publications team and to Paul O'Connor for continuing to provide the layout of these books to present Ringu Tulku's teachings accessibly to the reader. Thank you to the organisers of teachings we drew on for the content here, in particular, Dharma Convivium for the London teachings. And thank you to the organisers of the online Shedra course, where one section was included from, including Minna Stenroos.

Thank you to Robin Lipsey for the use of his barn where the White Tara Group meets. Thank you to the teams at Holy Isle, Scotland, and at

The Abbey, Oxfordshire, where much of this volume was written up and where the conducive environments helped focus the book to take shape.

Thank you to Ringu Tulku for providing such endless, patient and kind teaching along our paths, for all of our journeys 'from head to heart'. May we all arrive ... one day at a time.

Mary Heneghan
On behalf of Bodhicharya Publications
Oxford, April 2013

Information about the White Tara Group, as well as other Bodhicharya groups, can be found on the Groups page at www.bodhicharya.org. As can further information on the Bodhicharyavatara online Shedra teachings.

About the Author

Ringu Tulku Rinpoche is a Tibetan Buddhist Master of the Kagyu Order. He was trained in all schools of Tibetan Buddhism under many great masters including HH the 16th Gyalwang Karmapa and HH Dilgo Khyentse Rinpoche. He took his formal education at Namgyal Institute of Tibetology, Sikkim and Sampurnananda Sanskrit University, Varanasi, India. He served as Tibetan Textbook Writer and Professor of Tibetan Studies in Sikkim for 25 years.

Since 1990, he has been travelling and teaching Buddhism and meditation in Europe, America, Canada, Australia and Asia. He participates in various interfaith and 'Science and Buddhism' dialogues and is the author of several books on Buddhist topics. These include *Path to Buddhahood, Daring Steps, The Ri-me Philosophy of Jamgon Kongtrul the Great, Confusion Arises as Wisdom*, the *Lazy Lama* series and the *Heart Wisdom* series, as well as several children's books, available in Tibetan and European languages.

He founded the organisations Bodhicharya - see www.bodhicharya.org and Rigul Trust - see www.rigultrust.org.

Other books by Ringu Tulku

ALSO PUBLISHED BY BODHICHARYA PUBLICATIONS:
THE LAZY LAMA SERIES.

- *Buddhist Meditation*
- *The Four Noble Truths*
- *Refuge: Finding a Purpose and a Path*
- *Bodhichitta: Awakening Compassion and Wisdom*
- *Living without Fear and Anger*

PUBLISHED BY SHAMBHALA:

- *Path to Buddhahood:* Teachings on Gampopa's 'Jewel Ornament of Liberation'
- *Daring Steps:* Traversing the Path of the Buddha
- *Mind Training*
- *The Ri-Me Philosophy of Jamgon Kongtrul the Great:* A Study of the Buddhist Lineages of Tibet.
- *Confusion Arises as Wisdom:* Gampopa's Heart Advice on the Path of Mahamudra.

PUBLISHED BY RIGUL TRUST:

Chenrezig: The Practice of Compassion
A Commentary

PUBLISHED BY FINDHORN PRESS:

The Boy who had a Dream
An illustrated book for children
Available from Rigul Trust at www.rigultrust.org

For an up to date list of books by Ringu Tulku, please see the Books section at

www.bodhicharya.org

All proceeds received by Bodhicharya Publications from the sale of this book go direct to humanitarian and educational projects because the work involved in producing this book has been given free of charge.